Stundenblätter
Aldous Huxley
"Brave New World"

Ingrid Sonnhütter

Stundenblätter
Aldous Huxley
"Brave New World"

24 Seiten Beilage

Ernst Klett Verlag für Wissen und Bildung
Stuttgart · Dresden

Reihe: Stundenblätter Englisch

Eine Taschenbuchausgabe des Romans liegt vor:
Aldous Huxley, Brave New World
Published by Triad Grafton, London/Glasgow/Toronto/Sydney/Auckland
ISBN 0 586 04434 5

Nach dieser Ausgabe wird im Stundenblätterheft zitiert.
Sie ist als Klettbuch 57766 erhältlich.

Die Deutsche Bibliothek – CIP-Einheitsaufnahme

Sonnhütter, Ingrid:
Stundenblätter Aldous Huxley „Brave New World" / Ingrid Sonnhütter. –
5. Aufl. – Stuttgart; Dresden: Klett, Verlag für Wissen und Bildung, 1993
  (Reihe: Stundenblätter Englisch)
  ISBN 3-12-925111-1

5. Auflage 1993
Alle Rechte vorbehalten
Fotomechanische Wiedergabe nur mit Genehmigung des Verlages
© Ernst Klett Verlag für Wissen und Bildung GmbH, Stuttgart 1983
Satz: G. Müller, Heilbronn
Druck: Wilhelm Röck, Weinsberg. Printed in Germany.
Einbandgestaltung: Zembsch' Werkstatt, München
ISBN 3-12-925111-1

Inhalt

Einleitung

Schwerpunkte der Interpretation

"Multiplying our possible futures is important; but these images need to be organized, crystallized into structured form. In the past, utopian literature did this for us. It played a practical, crucial role in ordering man's dreams about alternative futures." (Alvin Toffler, Future Shock, p. 421) So begründet Toffler das Interesse der Menschen an der literarischen Utopie. Wie kaum ein anderes Werk dieser Art weist Huxleys "Brave New World" die wesentlichen Strukturmerkmale der literarischen Utopie, die sich herauskristallisieren lassen, in beispielhafter Weise auf:

— Geschichtslosigkeit und räumliche Isolation
— Stabilität im Sinne eines „allgemeinen Consensus über die geltenden Werte" (Dahrendorf, S. 332) oder auch das, was Alvin Toffler als "static societies" (Toffler, p. 421) bezeichnet.
— Das Fehlen jeglicher Konflikte und somit das Verschmelzen des Einzelnen mit der Gemeinschaft als Folge des „allgemeinen" – in der Regel erzwungenen – „Consensus". "All Utopias are anti-individualist and all their levelling sacrifices the person". (Ionesco, Of Utopianism and Intellectuals, p. 36)

"Community – Identity – Stability", das Motto von Huxleys Schöner Neuer Welt, könnte also mit gutem Recht über vielen anderen literarischen Utopien stehen.
In seinem Essayband "Brave New World Revisited" (1958) geht Huxley noch einmal kritisch auf die Techniken ein, mit deren Hilfe die komplexe Sozialstruktur seines totalitären Weltstaats aufrecht erhalten wird, und analysiert die Theorie, die dem Roman zugrundeliegt. Der neue Mensch in BNW, seine ethischen und moralischen Vorstellungen, seine Integration in das Staatsgebilde, sein Sozialverhalten und letztendlich seine vollständige Entmündigung werden möglich gemacht durch zwei Manipulationsinstrumente, denen auch Huxley in seiner Reflexion über den Roman breiten Raum gegeben hat:

a) Sprache
b) Gentechnik

"In their anti-rational propaganda the enemies of freedom systematically pervert the resources of language in order to wheedle or stampede their victims into thinking, feeling and acting as they, the mind-manipulators, want them to think, feel and act. An education for freedom... must be, among other things, an education in the proper uses of language." (Huxley, "Brave New World Revisited", p. 146/147). In dem Kapitel "Education for Freedom" (BNW Revisited) weist Huxley nachdrücklich auf den Zusammenhang von Sprache und Denken hin. Sprache kann einerseits zum gefährlichen Propaganda-, Macht- und Manipulationsinstrument werden, andrerseits jedoch zum einzig probaten Mittel der Erziehung zu Kritikfähigkeit, Rationalität und Toleranz: "Man's progress from animality to civilization" ("Brave New World Revisited", p. 145) Betrachten wir die Gesellschaft von BNW unter diesem Aspekt, so wird deutlich, daß Begriffe wie Religion, Glück, Liebe, Kunst und Wissenschaft nur noch als sprachliche Hülsen weiterbestehen und daß sie vollständig in den Dienst des Systems genommen wurden. Hand in Hand mit dem Verfall der Begriffe

geht der Verfall der dahinterstehenden Werte. In seinem Bemühen, uns auf die Gefahren der Manipulation durch Sprache hinzuweisen, sollte Huxley, einige Jahre später, von Orwell und seiner Konstruktion des "Newspeak" in „1984" unterstützt werden:
"Don't you see, that the whole aim of Newspeak is to narrow the range of thought? In the end we shall make thoughtcrime literally impossible, because there will be no words in which to express it." (Orwell, 1984, p. 45).

Um ein Volk von willfährigen Sklaven zu schaffen ("people"... who... "love their servitude", Vorwort zu "BNW", p. 14), ist das Instrument „Sprache" unerläßlich, um Denken und Verhalten manipulieren zu können. Ist die „Suggestionstechnik" (Vorwort zu "BNW", p. 15) erst einmal derart perfektioniert wie in "Brave New World", fehlt zur vollständigen Entmündigung ihrer Bürger nur noch *ein* weiteres Element, das zur Zeit, als Huxley den Roman schrieb, mit vollem Recht noch als utopisch bezeichnet werden mußte und das heutzutage in bedenkliche, ja unheimliche Nähe gerückt ist: "a foolproof system of eugenics, designed to standardize the human product" (Vorwort zu "BNW", p. 15):

„In 1931, when Brave New World was being written, I was convinced that there was still plenty of time." So beginnt Huxley seine Romananalyse "Brave New World Revisited" im Jahre 1958. Inzwischen sind weitere vierundzwanzig Jahre vergangen, die uns Huxleys Schreckensvision noch ein gutes Stück näher gebracht haben. Die künstliche Erzeugung und das Klonen (Erklärung siehe unten) von Menschen, gezielte Eingriffe in das Erbmaterial und genetische Manipulationen, waren 1931 noch Fiktion, und auch 1958 lagen solche Vorstellungen noch außerhalb des Möglichen. Erst in den letzten zehn Jahren ist die "Gentechnologie" als Teilbereich der Humanbiologie verstärkt ins öffentliche Interesse gerückt.

Kurz gesagt bedeutet „Gentechnik" den Eingriff in die menschliche (pflanzliche / tierische) Erbsubstanz mit dem Ziel, diese zu verändern. Das Verfahren der sogenannten „Geningenieure" bis ins einzelne nachzuvollziehen, ist für einen Laien schwierig, dennoch kann man sich mit Hilfe zahlreicher populärwissenschaftlicher Darstellungen über Ablauf und eventuelle Folgen der wissenschaftlichen Experimente informieren.

Wenn im folgenden einige Problembereiche und Verfahrensweisen der Gentechnologie kurz skizziert werden, so erhebt diese Darstellung selbstverständlich keinen Anspruch auf Vollständigkeit oder wissenschaftliche Genauigkeit. Ihr Ziel ist nur, dem Lehrer einige Hintergrundinformation zu liefern, die Huxleys Vision aus dem Jahre 1931 in ein beängstigend aktuelles Licht rücken.

Wie jede hochentwickelte Wissenschaft, ist auch die „Gentechnik" stark spezialisiert und läßt sich, je nach Ziel, in verschiedene Bereiche aufteilen:

☐ *Die Gentechnik zur Herstellung von Medikamenten und Hormonen*

Um die Gentechnik kommerziell nutzbar zu machen und große Mengen von Medikamenten wie Wachstumshormone, Insulin etc. herzustellen, wird die Geninformation (Chromosomen), die sich im Innern eines Zellkerns befindet, mit Hilfe von Scherenenzymen entnommen und ins Innere eines Virus eingesetzt. Der Virus wiederum wird auf ein Bakterium angesetzt und „entleert" seinen Inhalt in das Bakterium. Diese mit fremdem Genmaterial gespeisten Bakterien vermehren sich, bilden ganze Bakterienstämme, und stellen auf diese Weise die verschiedenen biologischen Wirkstoffe in beliebiger Menge her. In den USA gibt es bereits chemische Betriebe, die sich ausschließlich mit dieser Art der Produktion von Medikamenten befassen.

☐ *Gentechnik und Umweltschutz*

Durch ein Verschmelzen der Zellkerne von Pflanzen kann man die Erbinformation zweier Pflanzen kombinieren und erhält somit Mischformen. (z. B. Tomaten und Kartoffeln). Genetisch umkonstruierte Nutzpflanzen dieser Art oder auch genetisch umkonstruierte Mikroorganismen zur Energiegewinnung, Umweltentgiftung etc., verweisen auf mögliche positive Aspekte der Genforschung.

□ *Gentechnik zur Manipulation der menschlichen Erbsubstanz*

Insgesamt eröffnet die Molekularbiologie sowohl erschreckende als auch hoffnungsvolle Perspektiven. Die Reduzierung des Menschen auf eine bestimmte Kombination von Chemikalien läßt erhebliche soziale und politische Folgen befürchten. So weist Jost Herbig zurecht auf den „primitiven molekulargenetischen Positivismus" mancher Genforscher hin und warnt vor den unübersehbaren Folgen einer „Menschenzucht". Als – nicht mehr rein fiktive – Schreckensvision wären etwa folgende Verfahrensweisen denkbar:

– Sterilisation der als genetisch „minderwertig" erachteten Bevölkerungsgruppen
– künstliche Befruchtung mit dem in Samenbanken aufbewahrten Sperma ausgesucht „hochwertiger" Erbsubstanzträger
– biochemische Veränderung der menschlichen Erbsubstanz
– und schließlich das sogenannte „Klonen": ein Verfahren, dessen Ziel es ist, identische, genormte Lebewesen aus einer Eizelle hervorzubringen.

Der Versuch wurde bereits erfolgreich an Fröschen und vor drei Jahren auch an Mäusen unternommen. Vereinfacht dargestellt geht man dabei folgendermaßen vor: Das Ei des Froschweibchens wird zunächst geleert, bis nur noch die Schale der Eizelle übrig ist. Dann wird einer Kaulquappe ein Stück Gewebe entnommen. Die Erbinformation dieser entnommenen Zelle wird mit Hilfe einer Glaskanüle ins Innere der geleerten Eizelle eingepflanzt. Da sich die Eizelle als einzige

Zelle von selbst vermehrt, ist damit bereits der Prozeß eingeleitet, der die identischen Wesen (in diesem Fall Frösche) hervorbringt. Obgleich das Verfahren bei Säugetieren sehr viel schwieriger ist, wurde auch dieser Schritt schon getan (Mäuse).

Es ist wohl nur einem kleinen Kreis von Wissenschaftlern möglich zu sagen, ob das Klonen von Menschen, also Huxleys "Bokanovsky-Gruppen", in greifbare Nähe gerückt ist, oder ob wir dem Autor zustimmen können, wenn er, ebenfalls im Jahre 1958, rückblickend auf den Roman, die doch einigermaßen beruhigende Äußerung tut: "Babies in bottles and the centralized control of reproduction are not perhaps impossible; but it is quite clear that for a long time to come we shall remain a viviparous species breeding at random." (Brave New World Revisited, p. 13)

Zur Konzeption der Unterrichtseinheit

Bei der Schwerpunktbildung für die Unterrichtseinheit wurden die auf S. 7f. vorgestellten Problemstellungen zugrunde gelegt.

Die gesamte Unterrichtseinheit ist in vier Sequenzen aufgeteilt:

Sequenz 1 umfaßt nur eine Unterrichtsstunde, die zur Interpretation des Romans hinführt und den Schülern die notwendigen Informationen über den Autor, die literarische Gattung und die historische Einordnung des Werks vermittelt.

Sequenz 2 umfaßt drei Stunden. In diesen drei Stunden soll versucht werden, den Schülern die beiden Macht- und Manipulationsinstrumente des Huxleyschen Weltstaates, Konditionierung und Hypnopädie, vor Augen zu führen, wobei es unerläßlich ist, den real existierenden theoretischen Hintergrund dieser Manipulationstechniken durch Zusatztexte und Zusatzinformationen zu erläutern.

Sequenz 3, "BNW's Ideology", geht über sechs Stunden und untersucht den ideologischen Überbau des Gesellschaftsmodells. In dieser Sequenz wird vor allem das gefährliche Manipulationsinstrument der *Sprache* thematisiert, das durch Aushöhlen von Begriffen und damit verbunden der Pervertierung aller Werte die Brave New Worlder auch der letzten potentiellen Möglichkeit, unabhängiges Denken zu entwickeln, beraubt. *Sequenz 4* schließlich zeigt den Menschen im Konflikt mit einem nahezu „perfekten" System, dessen Unmenschlichkeit und sanftes Grauen nur durch das „Fehlverhalten" einiger Eindringlinge und Außenseiter bewußt gemacht werden kann. Auch die 14./ 15. Stunde, die noch einmal auf den Roman als Ganzes und Huxleys eigene (nachträgliche) Stellungnahme eingehen, lassen sich als Auseinandersetzung des Autors und des Lesers mit der satirischen und abschreckenden Darstellung einer denkbaren Gesellschaftsform unter diesen Aspekt subsumieren.

Bei jeder Romanbehandlung in der Schule gibt es prinzipiell zwei Möglichkeiten. Entweder wird der Text vorher ausgeteilt und ist zu Beginn der Besprechung von allen Schülern gelesen, oder er wird in der ersten Stunde ausgegeben und dann kapitelweise durchgearbeitet. Da die Romananalyse in unserem Fall nicht kursorisch vorgeht, sondern Schwerpunkte bildet, sollten alle Schüler den Roman zuvor gelesen haben und zusätzlich die jeweils behandelten Kapitel gründlich vorbereiten.

Bestimmte Schwierigkeiten, die bei der Behandlung einer Ganzschrift in der Schule auftauchen, verstärken sich im Fremdsprachenunterricht. So z.B. die Fragen: Welche Stoffmengen können die Schüler bewältigen? Wovon muß der Lehrer – realistischerweise – ausgehen? Wieviel Raum soll der rein sprachlichen Bewältigung (Übersetzung, Grammatik etc.) des Textes eingeräumt werden? Welches Lernziel steht im Vordergrund? Die inhaltliche Interpretation? Die Verbesserung der Sprechfähigkeit? Die Diskussionsbereitschaft der Schüler untereinander? Die Schulung der schriftlichen Ausdrucksfähigkeit?

Das methodische Vorgehen, das ich gewählt habe, hängt von der Beantwortung dieser Fragen und der daraus resultierenden Prioritäten ab:

Zur ersten und zweiten Frage: insgesamt bewältigen die Schüler meist weniger, als der Lehrer annimmt, und man muß davon ausgehen, daß schwächere Schüler dem Unterrichtsgeschehen oft nur mit Mühe folgen können. Zusatzarbeiten wie Referate etc. sollten also möglichst den Schülern übergeben werden, die mit der häuslichen Lektüre der Ganzschrift nicht schon mehr als ausgelastet sind. Die rein sprachliche Bewältigung des Textes habe ich nur in den Klausuren berücksichtigt (Grammatikteil/Übersetzung), da mir zum einen das Einschieben von Grammatikeinheiten den Fluß der Unterrichtseinheit zu stören schien und sie zum andern ohne großen Arbeitsaufwand vom Lehrer selbst erstellt und ad libitum eingefügt werden können.

Die Frage nach dem übergeordneten Lernziel ist letztlich nur subjektiv zu beantworten: der Idealfall einer sinnvollen Behandlung eines so umstrittenen und brisanten Thesenromans wie Huxleys "Brave New World" wäre sicherlich, wenn die Sprech- und Diskussionsbereitschaft der Schüler so groß wäre, daß der Lehrer nur sparsam in das Unterrichtsgeschehen eingreifen müßte. Dieser Idealfall ist natürlich eine Illusion, deshalb sollte das (schülerzentrierte) Unterrichtsgespräch, das fragend-entwickelnde Verfahren und somit das Fördern der Sprechfähigkeit im Vordergrund stehen. Als Gerüst hierfür sind die häufig sehr kleinschrittigen Inhalts- und Interpretationsfragen gedacht, die selbstverständlich – je nach Leistungsstand der Schüler – zusammengefaßt und abstrahiert werden können. Um den Ablauf der Stunden etwas aufzulockern, sind Kurzreferate, Still- und Gruppenarbeitsphasen vorgesehen, wobei man jedoch über Sinn und Unsinn der Gruppenarbeit im Fremdsprachenunterricht geteilter Meinung sein kann. Als eine Art *brainstorming* hat sie sicher auch hier ihre Berechtigung, kann jedoch bei dem übergeordneten Lernziel der (mündlichen und schriftlichen) Ausdrucksfähigkeit in der Fremdsprache nicht denselben Rang einnehmen wie im Deutsch- oder Geschichtsunterricht.

Zusammenfassend möchte ich noch einmal sagen, daß die vorliegende Unterrichtseinheit keinen weiteren Anspruch erhebt als den, Interpretationshilfe, Denkanstoß und Arbeitserleichterung zu sein und daß das methodische Hauptgewicht, aufgrund des übergeordneten Lernziels, *bewußt* auf das Unterrichtsgespräch gelegt wurde.

Zur Konzeption des Heftes

Um gewisse Mißverständnisse von vornherein auszuschalten, sollten zunächst zwei Dinge geklärt werden:

- Die detaillierte Ausarbeitung der Stunden ist weder Gängelung noch Patentrezept, sie soll vielmehr dem Lehrer Hilfen und Anregungen bieten und ihm die zweifellos sehr aufwendige Vorbereitung einer fremdsprachlichen Ganzschrift etwas erleichtern.
- Ich habe diese Unterrichtseinheit parallel in zwei Leistungskursen Englisch durchgeführt, habe sie also bereits praktisch erprobt. Selbstverständlich tauchten Schwierigkeiten auf, selbstverständlich ließ sich nicht alles wie geplant durchführen. Dennoch meine ich, daß der vorliegende Interpretationsansatz – cum grano salis – methodisch und didaktisch zu vertreten, und, nach eigenem Gutdünken, zu „gebrauchen" ist: "you pays your money and you takes your choice".

a) Der Fremdsprachenunterricht in der gymnasialen Oberstufe wird zu 9/10 in der Fremdsprache abgehalten. Interpretationsklausuren, Textanalysen etc. müssen von den Schülern ebenfalls in der Fremdsprache geschrieben werden. Daraus folgt zweierlei: zum einen wird die literarische Interpretation an der Schule weniger wissenschaftlich und von einfacherer Struktur als an der Universität sein, zum andern muß der speziell fremdsprachliche Wortschatz zu Inhaltsanalyse und Interpretation des entsprechenden literarischen Werks verfügbar sein. Sollen dem Lehrer die Stundenblätter also eine wirkliche Hilfe sein, müssen inhaltliche Hinweise in der Fremdsprache gegeben werden.

Nun weist ein fremdsprachlicher Text, der von einem *non-native speaker* verfaßt wurde, natürlich stilistische Mängel auf, die auch eine Korrektur durch einen *native speaker* nicht ganz beheben kann. Ich bin mir über dieses Manko durchaus im klaren, nehme es aber aus den oben genannten Gründen in Kauf.

Die methodisch-didaktischen Überlegungen zum Verlauf der Stunden ebenfalls in der Fremdsprache anzustellen, schien mir dagegen überflüssig, da diese Überlegungen ja im Unterricht nicht versprachlicht werden. Deshalb also die etwas „unreine" Mischform aus zwei Sprachen.

Darstellung der Unterrichtseinheit

Sequenz 1: Introduction

1. Stunde:
Information about the Author and the Literary Genre

Zur didaktischen Funktion

Geht man von der Voraussetzung aus, daß die Schüler den Roman gelesen haben, kann man sie in dem kurzen einführenden Gespräch durchaus schon nach ihrem spontanen Urteil fragen, ohne dabei allzuviel von der Interpretation vorwegzunehmen.

Die Frage nach Huxleys Biographie und weiteren Werken leitet nahtlos über zu der Hektographie (vgl. S. 13), die den Schülern genauere Informationen über Leben und Werk des Autors geben soll. In der Zusammenfassung (bzw. dem Herausgreifen der wichtigsten Punkte) sollte vor allem noch einmal auf Huxleys familiären Hintergrund, seine umfassende Bildung und den geistreich-zynischen Stil der meisten seiner Romane eingegangen werden. Es wäre unter Umständen auch interessant herauszufinden, weshalb Huxleys literarischer Ruhm in seiner zweiten Lebenshälfte mit Romanen wie "Ape and Essence" oder "The Genius and the Goddess" merklich sinkt.

Ein zweiter wichtiger Schwerpunkt dieser Einführungsstunde ist die Definition der literarischen Begriffe „Utopie" bzw. „Dystopie". Das Wort „Dystopie" – das Huxleys Roman genau beschreibt – ist eine neuere Schöpfung, und man ging dabei von der Annahme aus, daß der Begriff „Utopie" ebensogut aus dem Griechischen u (=nicht) und topos (=Platz) wie auch „eutopia" (=der gute Ort) hervorgegangen sein könnte. Dystopia (=der schlechte Ort) wäre also somit als Gegensatz zu Eutopia zu verstehen. Die Diskussion dieser literarischen Begriffe läßt sich in zwei Teilbereiche untergliedern:

1. Die Frage nach Sinn und Zweck des Zukunftsromans überhaupt:
   – Warum werden Utopien geschrieben?
   – Was stört an positiven Utopien?
   – Weshalb ist die Dystopie die literarisch überzeugendere Form?
   – Was sind die Merkmale einer Utopie?
2. Die *literarische Tradition* der Utopie oder des Staatsromans, wobei das Schwergewicht sinnvollerweise auf die englische Tradition gelegt werden müßte.

Als abschließender Aspekt, der die Stunde abrundet und wieder zum Ausgangspunkt zurückführt, wird der Titel des Buches: „Wackere / schöne / gute?" neue Welt? genauer besprochen. Huxleys satirisches Shakespeare-Zitat ist inzwischen als geflügeltes Wort in die englische Sprache eingegangen und drückt genau die Zweifel aus, die dem Leser schon zu Beginn des ersten Kapitels an dieser „glücklichen", „erstrebenswerten" neuen Welt kommen und die *nach* der Lektüre – in Huxleys Sinne – als Abscheu und Warnung vor der beginnenden Dekadenz einer Massengesellschaft empfunden werden.

Ziele der Stunde

Die Schüler sollen
– über den biographischen Hintergrund Huxleys informiert werden

Aldous Huxley

Aldous Leonard Huxley, a grandson of Thomas Huxley, the famous biologist and friend of Charles Darwin, and a great nephew of Matthew Arnold, was born at Godalming, Surrey, on July 26, 1894. He was educated at Eton and, after an eye affliction had nearly blinded him, at Oxford, where he took a degree in English literature. His official introduction into the literary world of London came in 1919 when he joined the editorial staff of *The Athenaeum* under the sponsorship of J. Middleton Murry. As soon as his writing permitted he made his home in Italy or Southern France, and from 1937 to his death in 1963 lived in California, USA.

After publishing considerable poetry and some experimental prose, Huxley published his first novel, *Crome Yellow,* in 1921. Two other well-known novels followed in the 1920's, *Antic Hay* (1923) and *Point Counter Point* (1928). These novels won for Huxley a popular reputation as a cynical wit; they dazzled by the stylistic brilliance with which Huxley, tongue in cheek, evoked a sick glamour from the decadent and morally chaotic society that filled his pages. Having satirically anatomized what he presented as contemporary society in *Point Counter Point* and the earlier novels, he turned in *Brave New World* (1932) to an imaginative analysis of the future as it appeared to him already implicit in the present.

Always the moralist, Huxley wrote on the assumption that literature belongs in the market place not so much as commodity but as an arbitrating voice in the clamorous and confused dialogue between men and the ideas and ideals that would claim their allegiance. His persistent concern with the dangers of moral anarchy in a scientific and technological civilization was marked in all his novels and was given more explicit expression in such discursive writings as *Proper Studies (1927), Science, Liberty and Peace* (1946), *The Doors of Perception* (1954) and *Brave New World Revisited* (1958).

In *Ape and Essence* (1948), *The Genius and the Goddess* (1955) and *Island* (1962), Huxley turned again to two specific and recurrent preoccupations – the possibly disastrous consequences for mankind of rapidly acquired scientific power and the problems arising out of the hyperdevelopment of the intellect at the expense of other human qualities. If these later novels have failed to affect Huxley's critical reputation very much one way or another, this is perhaps due to the fact that Huxley's wit is not in itself sufficient to lend brilliance to concepts and concerns now so much traded upon in the small marketplaces of the intellect, perhaps to the fact that preoccupation with them seems to have bred increasing impatience with craftsmanship, or perhaps to the fact that one had learned all too well to anticipate Huxley at his own game.

Huxley belonged essentially to that peculiar breed known as "men of letters", writers with a wide range of interests who express themselves with facility in a variety of forms. The contribution of such men is difficult to assess, but it seems likely that as a fiction writer Huxley will survive as part of the essential atmosphere of a fascinating decade, the 1920's, and, possibly, as the author of *Brave New World*.

Insight II. Analyses of Modern British Literature, ed. by John v. Hagopian and Martin Dolch, Hirschgraben Verlag Frankfurt/M. 1971

- Intention und charakteristische Merkmale der (literarischen) Form der Utopie benennen können
- "BNW" in die Tradition der (englischen) Zukunftsromane einordnen können
- informiert werden, woher der Titel des Buches stammt und (evtl.) bereits auf die Spur gebracht werden, daß er hier satirisch gebraucht wird

Verlaufsskizze

Unterrichtsschritt 1:

In einem kurzen, einführenden Unterrichtsgespräch wird festgestellt, was die Schüler über den Autor und das Buch bereits wissen und wie sie es insgesamt beurteilen.

Unterrichtsschritt 2:

Den Schülern wird ein Text über Huxleys Leben und Werk (vgl. S. 13) ausgeteilt. Nach einer kurzen Lesephase sollten sie diesen Text entweder in einigen Sätzen zusammenfassen oder die Fakten notieren, die ihnen besonders wichtig erscheinen. (Siehe Fragen auf dem Stundenblatt)

Unterrichtsschritt 3:

a) In einem kurzen Lehrervortrag wird die literarische Form des Zukunftsromans besprochen und in groben Zügen an der Tafel festgehalten. (Siehe T. A.)
b) Außerdem soll versucht werden, den Schülern einen knappen geschichtlichen Abriß der (hauptsächlich englischen) utopischen Literatur zu geben und "BNW" in dieses Raster einordnen. Die wichtigsten Daten werden den Schülern auf einer Hektographie (vgl. S. 16) ausgeteilt.

Unterrichtsschritt 4:

Ohne allzuviel vorwegzunehmen, sollen sich die Schüler in Stillarbeit überlegen, was ihnen zum Titel des Buches einfällt (Übersetzung, Assoziationen, Bezug: Titel – Inhalt etc.) Das Ergebnis der Stillarbeit wird besprochen und an der Tafel festgehalten. (Siehe T. A.)

Zusätzliche Diskussionspunkte

Es können einzelne Schüler in Form von Kurzreferaten über die verschiedenen Utopien und utopischen Romane berichten. Besonders interessant wäre natürlich ein Vergleich mit Orwells „1984".

Zum Inhalt der Stunde

Unterrichtsschritt 3a:
Utopia – dystopia

The word "utopia" goes back to Sir Thomas More's novel "Utopia", and, literally translated, it means: "not-place" (Greek: u – not; topos – place). Not-place might be a place, that does *not yet* exist, or that can never exist because man is unable to reach perfection or endure cruel tyranny for ever.
Whereas the utopian novels of the early Renaissance, especially More's "Utopia" and Bacon's "New Atlantis", are still marked by the authors' faith in science, reason, and progress, the 17th and 18th century novels, like Hall's "Mundus Alter et Idem" or Swift's "Gulliver's Travels" are already characterized by the authors' pessimistic and cynical view of man.
So it's all the more astonishing that the word "dystopia", used as a literary category, is only a fairly recent creation, based on the assumption that the word "utopia" could also be traced back to the Greek root "eutopia" (= the good place), as opposed to "dystopia" (= the

bad place). This expression is now commonly used to describe negative utopias like "BNW" or "1984".

A further characterization of books like "BNW", "Gulliver's Travels", or "Mundus Alter et Idem" is the fact that they're satires, and could thus be described as "satirical dystopias". (Satire – see also lesson 14).

In a lecture he held in 1978, Hugh Silverman (c.f. reference books) even created the term "Heterotopia", merging the elements of "utopia" and "dystopia" into a new concept that might be described as a sociological blueprint the realistic elements of which can be considered as a model.

Unterrichtsschritt 3 b:
History of the literary genre

Even though the name of "utopia" was first used in the year 1516, the literary genre as such has a long tradition and can be traced back as far as the ancient descriptions of paradise in the Epic of Gilgamesh, and the description of the Elysian Fields in Homer's "Odyssey". The first to add an element of political theory, however, was Plato in his "Republic" ("Politeia") (427–347 B.C.): Plato's "Republic" is based on the idea of justice. Justice is made up of three virtues: wisdom, valour and temperance. This principle is transferred to the organization of the "Republic", and thus Plato establishes three ranks: the highest rank are the Kings or philosophers who govern the State wisely (=wisdom); the second rank are the warriors who bravely defend their State (= valour); the third rank are the peasants, fishermen, mariners and the tradesmen who calmly and moderately provide food and nourishment (= temperance). Plato's "Republic" can in fact be called the model for all the other utopias that were written in the course of many centuries. As we can't possibly give a complete survey of the general history of utopias, we'll concentrate on a few landmarks in the history of English

utopias finally leading up to Huxley's "BNW".

The 16ᵗʰ and 17ᵗʰ centuries (the Renaissance):
The novel that gave its name to the literary genre, Sir Thomas More's "Utopia" (1516), was not published in English but in Latin. The fantastic traveller's tales of Pliny and Lucian might have suggested the literary form of "Utopia", i.e. a student of philosophy (Hythlodaeus) travelling to an imaginary place and telling other people about it. First of all Raphael Hythlodaeus talks about the geographical situation of the island "Utopia"; then he describes the government, social life, laws, military institutions and religion. Even though "Utopia" might seem anything but a perfect society to us (no privacy, very limited personal liberty, a strictly patriarchal character and severe punishment for petty crimes), we must not forget that Tudor England (especially under the tyranny of Henry VIII) did not even enjoy the basic civic rights like freedom of speech and thought, or social justice, and that More himself was executed because he refused to deny papal authority and because he did not agree to Henry's divorce of Catharine of Aragon. It's mainly because of its realism and precision, its vivacity and poetry, as seen against the politically menacing background of Tudor England, that More's 'Utopia' remains a classical blueprint of a perfectly organized state.

The three best-known utopian novels of the Renaissance are More's "Utopia", Campanella's "Civitas Solis" and Francis Bacon's "New Atlantis". Let's now have a look at the last one.

Francis Bacon's "New Atlantis" was published in 1627 and remained a fragment. It continues the tradition of the fantastic traveller's tales that were particularly popular in the 17ᵗʰ and 18ᵗʰ centuries. The "house of Salomon" on the island of "Bensalem" can well be compared to Plato's philosopher Kings,

15

The most important landmarks in the history of the utopian novel (in Britain)

427–347 B. C. (Plato)
In his "Politeia" ("Republic") Plato describes some form of ideal state, based on the idea of justice
model for all the later utopias

1516: Sir Thomas More – published his novel "Utopia" (in Latin) that gave its name to the literary genre. It's in the tradition of Pliny's and Lucian's fantastic traveller's tales.
1627: Francis Bacon's "New Atlantis" continues the tradition of the fantastic traveller's tales, and shows Bacon's faith in the blessings of science.
1605: With his book *"Mundus Alter et Idem"* ("Another World and yet the Same") *Joseph Hall* invented a subspecies of the genre, i. e. the satirical dystopia. He satirizes all kinds of human vices and follies.
1727: Swift's "Gulliver's Travels" is another bitter attack on human vices. In his four journeys to distant parts of the earth, Gulliver discovers four different kinds of civilization, and comes to the conclusion that human beings are the the "most pernicious race of little odious vermin that nature ever suffered to crawl upon the surface of the earth".
1872 Samuel Butler's "Erewhon" (an anagram of the word "nowhere") with its inhabitants' worship of success and physical beauty, and their regressive hate of machines, is an ironical mirror of late Victorian society.
1905: In his novel *"A Modern Utopia", H. G. Wells* describes a technical world-state, governed by efficient managers. A book that shows Wells's optimistic belief in the positive development of civilization and technology, whereas the same author presents a fantastic but abhorring prospect of the future in his famous novel *"The Time Machine"*.
1932: Huxley's "Brave New World"
1959: Huxley's "Brave New World Revisited" – Essays on 'BNW'
1948 George Orwell publishes his famous novel *"1984"* in which after the experience of the Second World War he describes the miserable life of an impoverished people that is cruelly suppressed by an omnipotent political Party.

---

and the description of all kinds of technical inventions shows Bacon's faith in the blessings of science, and his wish to accord a high standard of technology and science with the traditional ethical and social norms.

With his book *"Mundus Alter et Idem"* ("Another World and yet the same", or: "The Discovery of a New World" – 1605) *Joseph Hall* had invented a new subspecies of the genre, i. e. the satirical dystopia. He ridicules the popular traveller's tales and satirizes all kinds of vices and folly. For this purpose he invents a map of fictitious countries, each of which is "ruled" by one principal vice. So, for instance "Pamphagonia", the land of gluttony, or "Yvronia", the realm of inebriety. Hall's satire is still rather cheerful and does not yet foreshadow the bitter cynicism and horror of Huxley and Orwell, nor even the savage criticism of:

Swift's "Gulliver's Travels" (1727)
In his four journeys to distant parts of the earth, Gulliver discovers four different kinds of civilization, most of which are the object of a bitter attack on human vices, For all their redeeming features, the Lilliputians (a people of tiny dwarfs) prove susceptible to intrigue and narrow-mindedness. Brobding-nag, the next country he finds himself in, is a country of giants, where Gulliver is exposed to constant peril and suffers from the coarse-ness of his hosts. The island of Balnibarbi is a colony of Laputa, a people of theoreticians who are only interested in music and mathe-matics, but are absolutely unable to do any-thing practical. From Laputa Gulliver travels to two other islands, and, in the year 1710, starts on his last trip to the land of the Houyhnhnms. The Houyhnhnms reign over the disgusting, ape-like men called Yahoos; they look like horses and live together in a to-tally rational, ideal form of society. When he finally returns home after his adventures, Gulliver is convinced of what Swift wanted to show us in his satire, i. e. that human beings are "the most pernicious race of little odious vermin that nature ever suffered to crawl upon the surface of the earth" (the King of Brobdingnag).

Another distopian satire in the history of the English Utopia is:
Samuel Butler's "Erewhon" (1872)
The title of the book is an anagram of the word "nowhere", but the utopian elements are confined to the Erewhonians' physical beauty, grace, and health. Their worship of success, their regressive hate of machines, and their strange ideas about diseases and immorality, together with the self-satisfied priggishness of the typically Victorian pro-tagonist constitute an ironical reflection of late Victorian society.
Although the tradition of Utopian novels in Great Britain goes back as far as 1516, the Utopian novels most of use are familiar with, are those of the 20th century. We'll mainly have to consider the novels Huxley himself knew, mentioned and satirized. Particularly two well-known novels by H. G. Wells (1866–1946): One of them is "A Modern Utopia" (1905) where Wells describes a World-State ruled by technology and govern-ed by efficient managers, the so-called 'Sam-urai'. It has often been said that Huxley's board of World Controllers and the repul-sive, over-technicized Brave New World was a bitter satire on Well's optimistic belief in the positive development of civilization and technology. In "The Time Machine", an-other novel by the same author, Wells describ-es a machine that allows its inventor to inve-stigate the fourth dimension, i.e. to move backwards or forwards through the centuries. With his description of an over-civilized, dec-adent race, the Eloi, and their fierce oppo-nents, the Morlocks, Wells presents a fantas-tic but abhorrent prospect of the future of mankind.
The two outstanding utopian novels, how-ever, that contain all the negative possibilities of the 20th and the 21st centuries, are Hux-ley's "Brave New World" and Orwell's "1984". The 'Soft Gulag' of "Brave New World" as opposed to Orwell's description of the miserable life of an impoverished people, cruelly suppressed by an omnipotent political Party.

Unterrichtsschritt 4:
The title of the book

At first sight the title of the novel seems strangely inadequate. Why should a world like this be called "brave"? The modern meaning of the word would be something like "courageous". Well, courage is certainly not one of the Brave New Worlders' characteris-tics. So that brings us back to the old use of the word, which is "fine, splendid". The whole expression is a quotation from Shake-speare's "Tempest", when Miranda, Prospero's daughter, admires the result of her father's magical powers and exclaims with rapture: "O Brave New World that has such people in it!". Huxley used this quotation as a satirical parallel to the action of his novel: When John still lives on the Reservation, the only things he's familiar with, are a few of Shakespeare's plays, and Linda's enthusiastic description of a place called the civilized, the "brave" new world outside the Reservation. It's only when John has some acquaintance with this "wonderful" world, that he starts to use the adjective with the same disgust as the author.

Sequenz 2: The Instruments of Social Engineering in BNW

2. Stunde:
The "New" Man

Zur didaktischen Funktion

Die Analyse des Mottos, das nicht nur über der Menschenfabrik, sondern über dem ganzen Staatsgefüge steht, bietet einen interessanten Ansatzpunkt für die Betrachtung der Ideologie (siehe auch Sequenz 3), die dem System zugrunde liegt. Die Assoziationen, die der neue Slogan "Community- Identity- Stability" beim Leser weckt, erlauben außerdem einen vergleichenden Blick zurück in die alte, vergangene Welt.

Nach dieser eher abstrakten Hinführung zu Huxleys Gedankenwelt wenden wir uns der kalten, sterilen und künstlichen Atmosphäre der schönen neuen Welt zu, die auf den ersten Seiten des Romans eindringlich geschildert wird. Würde dem Leser nicht gleich zu Beginn der Hinweis gegeben, daß er sich in einer „Menschenfabrik" in London befindet, könnte er das hier beschriebene Gebäude auch für eine Leichenhalle halten. Dieses moderne Verwirrspiel, in dem Leben und Tod zu derselben Sterilität und Bedeutungslosigkeit abgesunken sind, ist bereits ein wichtiger Schlüssel zum Verständnis der schönen, neuen Welt und ihren Bürger.

Die „industrielle Fertigung" des Menschen, die es den Anführern und Kontrolleuren erlaubt, die Bevölkerung vom vorgeburtlichen Stadium an zu manipulieren, ist Voraussetzung und Grundlage für das Funktionieren des Staatsgebildes.

Wie nahe unsere moderne Welt den ehemals so utopisch klingenden Vorstellungen Huxleys gerückt ist, und welche Möglichkeiten die Erkenntnisse der Bio-Chemie und der Humanbiologie eröffnet haben, das mag die Information über den augenblicklichen Stand der Forschung (siehe Einleitung und Bibliographie) aufzeigen.

Ziele der Stunde

Die Schüler sollen
- das Motto "Community- Identity- Stability" (als Perversion der demokratischen Ideale: Freiheit – Gleichheit- Brüderlichkeit) in seiner Bedeutung für den Roman erkennen und analysieren können
- die Atmosphäre von Huxleys schöner, neuer Welt beschreiben können und evtl. Parallelen in unserer Welt sehen
- die einzelnen Schritte der künstlichen Herstellung von Menschen nachvollziehen können und die sozialpolitische Bedeutung des Bokanovsky-Verfahrens erkennen
- über die spektakulärsten genetischen Experimente in jüngster Zeit informiert werden und diese Information mit Huxleys Fiktion vergleichen

Verlaufsskizze

Voraussetzungen

Die Schüler haben das erste Kapitel gründlich gelesen.

Unterrichtsschritt 1:

Bevor man sich dem ersten Kapitel insgesamt zuwendet, wird zunächst das Motto: "Community- Identity- Stability" herausgegriffen. Um das Motto zu analysieren, sollten die Begriffe zunächst definiert werden. Im Anschluß daran läßt man die Schüler am besten frei äußern, was ihnen zu diesem Slogan einfällt. Die Ergebnisse werden an der Tafel festgehalten. (Siehe T. A.)

Unterrichtsschritt 2:

Nach der Analyse des Mottos überfliegen die Schüler den Text auf S. 19/20* (Beginn bis "…didn't occur to ask it.") noch einmal kurz. Im Anschluß daran wird im Unterrichtsgespräch der Gegensatz: Atmosphäre – Institution herausgearbeitet. (Kein T.A. vorgesehen)

Unterrichtsschritt 3:

Die Schüler halten die einzelnen Schritte der künstlichen Herstellung von Menschen, wie sie auf S. 21 ("still leaning…Bokanovsky's Process.") schriftlich (in Stichworten) fest und überlegen sich die Bedeutung dieses künstlichen Herstellungsprozesses. (Siehe T.A.)

Unterrichtsschritt 4:

Anhand des Textes (S. 21/22 "Bokanovsky's Process" bis S. 23 "…problem would be solved.") verschaffen sich die Schüler Klarheit über Ablauf und Bedeutung des Bokanovsky-Verfahrens. Im schülerzentrierten Unterrichtsgespräch wird noch einmal der Bezug:

'identity ← Bokanovsky's Process → social stability' hergestellt.

* Zitiert wird hier und im folgenden nach der Triad Grafton-Taschenbuchausgabe:
Aldous Huxley, Brave New World, published by Triad Grafton in 1990

Unterrichtsschritt 5:

Entweder in Form eines Schülerreferats oder in Form eines Lehrervortrags werden die Schüler über einige genetische Experimente informiert. Der augenblickliche Stand der Forschung wird anschließend mit der Schilderung in „BNW" verglichen.
(Informationen dazu vgl. S. 8/9)

Zusätzliche Diskussionspunkte

1) Gleichheit- Gleichmacherei- Identität
2) Wie wird – aufgrund der geschilderten Atmosphäre und der künstlichen Herstellung von Menschen – das Verhältnis der 'Brave New Worlder' zur Natur sein, und worin wird es sich äußern?
3) Genetische Manipulationen, eine Gefahr für die Menschheit?

Zum Inhalt der Stunde

Unterrichtsschritt 1:
The motto

Setting

In BNW the democratic ideals of liberty equality and fraternity have been converted to: identity- stability- community.
As we become more familiar with the political system of the world state, this transformation turns out to be explicable, even logical. *Community* as opposed to both individualism and fraternity prevents people from developing their own (individual and uncontrollable) ideas that might jeopardize the common beliefs. Community in BNW doesn't allow for any kind of dangerous solidarity (as implied by fraternity), which is also likely to menace the system.
One of the most important principles of BNW is *stability*. Freedom and stability seem incompatible; freedom implying non-conformity, movement and change, whereas stability and its connotations stand for an im-

pervious caste-system. (Connotations: immobility, rigidity, inflexibility).

The word *identity* hat two meanings: speaking of the identity of someone, we refer to a particular person as a unique being, to his characteristics and his personality. Apart from that, identity also means: absolute sameness, exact likeness. It doesn't, as yet, make sense to think of people as identical beings, and the step from equality to identity remains to be explained.

Unterrichtsschritt 2:
The atmosphere

Adjectives like "pale, white, dead, corpse-coloured, frozen" etc. would normally be found in the description of a morgue rather than a hatchery. The contrast between death, sterility, clinical atmosphere on the one hand, birth, fertility and newly-born-life on the other, suggests a mechanical, strangely artificial and highly standardized way of human production. A look at the "products" confirms this impression: "young, pink and callow students, eager to be as compliant as possible and willing to compose the backbone of society". (As expressed in the author's ironical description of their naive credulity: "straight from the horse's mouth / rare privilege" etc.) Ageless creatures that seem as artificial as their surroundings.

Unterrichtsschritt 3:
The artificial production of humans

The first step in the process is the operation that a carefully chosen female member of society undergoes voluntarily. Her ovary is taken out, preserved and developed. As soon as the eggs are ripe, they are separated, put into liquid and then carefully examined to prevent any kind of abnormal development. The actual fertilization process consists in dipping the eggs into a warm liquid that contains 'freeswimming spermatozoa'. As a last step, the eggs are put back into incubators, and are then separated according to their future caste. All the technical terms like "salinity, viscosity, incubators, receptacle" etc. make the description sound extremely convincing and genuine. *Reproduction,* a basic act and the symbol of nature, has been reduced to a highly complicated scientific process, with no human beings involved. Nature could only impair the smooth functioning of the system and must be looked upon as a potential enemy. (See also later: clothes etc.)

Unterrichtsschritt 4:
Bokanovsky's process

The result of Bokanovsky's Process is identity. In the process the development of Gamma, Delta and Epsilon eggs is checked while their number is increased, i. e. the substance that is sufficient for one normal adult, will now have to supply 96 identical beings; quantity at the expense of quality, "the principle of mass production applied to biology". Dozens of standardized human beings, whose IQ is kept below par. Has the old ideal of equality been achieved once and for all? Could identity be defined as the most perfect form of equality?

"Bokanovsky's Process is one of the major instruments of social stability." The DHC certainly has his reasons for saying so:

- As there's no difference between the individual human beings of one Bokanovsky Group, there's not even the chance of comparison and thus no reason for dissatisfaction.
- From the prenatal stage onwards, all lower caste individuals are conditioned to "like their unescapable social destiny" (see p. 31 heat conditioning, X-rays etc.).
- The different social castes are strictly separated, and the superiority or inferiority of the other castes is unquestioningly accepted by all of them.
- For all the slight differences that might

21

exist between the different Bokanovsky Groups, the fact remains that *one* group of (up to) 96 persons can be considered as *one* individual entity, and is thus infinitely malleable, the ideal "instrument of social stability".

"Happiness", another brick in the world state's ideological structure is already mentioned by the Director, and implicitly defined as the necessary result of perfect conditioning (see also later – conditioning should be conflict-proof) and as the inability to see beyond the "mental walls" of this conditioning. Breeding stupidity for the sake of "social stability" and "happiness". Is it "all too likely to come true"? We might be tempted to agree with Bertrand Russell's statement, if we look at some of the more recent experiments in genetics. (Siehe Einleitung)

3./4. Stunde:
Different Forms of Conditioning

Zur didaktischen Funktion

Nachdem sich die Schüler in der vorigen Stunde mit der künstlichen Erzeugung des Menschen und seiner vorgeburtlichen Prägung befaßt haben, soll ihnen nun im zweiten Kapitel ein mindestens ebenso wichtiges Stadium in der Programmierung des neuen Menschen bewußt gemacht werden: das Antrainieren konditionierter Reflexe und die Erziehung zum geforderten Klassenbewußtsein durch „Hypnopädie". Dabei soll vor allem das dahinter stehende behavioristische Verhaltensmodell analysiert werden, das für den gesamten Roman von zentraler Wichtigkeit ist. Eine weitergehende Information über die Theorie des Behaviorismus und dessen Ziele ist deshalb notwendig, weil Verhaltenstraining in „BNW" als ein weiteres zen-

trales Manipulationsinstrument eingesetzt wird.

Im Unterschied zu dieser Art von nonverbalem vorbewußten Verhaltenstraining muß die Anwendung der „Hypnopädie" als Verfeinerungsinstrument gesehen werden. Ihr Ziel ist es, die antrainierten Verhaltensweisen durch ein manipuliertes Bewußtsein zu stützen und zu festigen.

Es sollte den Schülern in dieser Doppelstunde nachdrücklich klargemacht werden, daß jegliche Art von unbewußter oder bewußter psychologischer ‚Programmierung' den Menschen zwar einerseits helfen kann, andererseits aber auch ein gefährliches und nur schwer kontrollierbares Manipulationsinstrument in den Händen der Anwender sein kann: "To the question 'quis custodiet custodes?' – who will mount guard over our guardians, who will engineer the engineers? – the answer is a bland denial that they need any supervision." (Huxley, Brave New World Revisited, p. 44)

Ziele der Stunde

Die Schüler sollen
– Ablauf und Ziel des Experiments in den "Neo-Pavlovian Conditioning Rooms" genau beschreiben können
– wissen, woher der Name "Neo-Pavlovian Conditioning Rooms" kommt und welches Experiment im Zusammenhang mit Pawlows Namen genannt wird
– mit Hilfe des Zusatztextes mit den Grundbegriffen des Behaviorismus vertraut gemacht werden
– durch ein Schülerreferat über Skinners behavioristischen Zukunftsroman "Futurum II" ("Walden Two") informiert werden (fakultativ)
– sich über Vorteile und Gefahren einer Verhaltensprogrammierung Gedanken machen

- erkennen, weshalb zwei verschiedene Verfahren angewandt werden (Konditionierung und Hypnopädie) und worin sie sich unterscheiden.

Verlaufsskizze

Voraussetzungen:
Die Schüler haben das Kapitel 2 gründlich gelesen und schriftlich zusammengefaßt.

Unterrichtsschritt 1:

Die Hausaufgabe (Summary von Kapitel 2) wird besprochen, wobei besonders auf das Experiment in den "Conditioning Rooms" hingewiesen wird.

Unterrichtsschritt 2:

In einem kurzen, lehrerzentrierten Unterrichtsgespräch wird die Herkunft des Wortes "Pavlovian" und die dahinter stehende Theorie des Behaviorismus kurz erläutert.

Unterrichtsschritt 3:

Die Schüler bekommen einen Text über die Grundbegriffe des Behaviorismus (siehe S. 25/26). Die Fragen zum Text werden in einer Phase der Stillarbeit (Gruppenarbeit) beantwortet, anschließend gemeinsam ausgewertet und an der Tafel festgehalten.

Unterrichtsschritt 4: (kann wegfallen)

Schülerreferat über Skinners "Walden Two", evtl. mit anschließender Diskussion über Vorzüge und Gefahren der behavioristischen Theorie (siehe Ergänzung).

Unterrichtsschritt 5:

a) Kapitel 2 (S. 41–43 von "Elementary class consciousness..." bis "...I've gone and woken the children.") wird laut gelesen, wobei besonders auf die Betonung der Slogans zu achten ist.
b) Daran schließt sich ein Unterrichtsgespräch über den Unterschied zwischen Konditionierung und Hypnopädie und die Bedeutung eines systemkonformen Klassenbewußtseins an. Die Ergebnisse dieses Unterrichtsgesprächs werden an der Tafel festgehalten.

Zusätzliche Diskussionspunkte

- Konditioniertes Verhalten – Fortschritt oder Gefahr?
- Ist Skinners Modell verlockend? Warum (nicht)?
- Vergleich: Hypnopädie – Hypnose – Gehirnwäsche etc.

Zum Inhalt der Stunde

Unterrichtsschritt 1:
The experiment in the Neo-Pavlovian conditioning rooms

In the first part of chapter 2, the students are shown how eight-month-old babies are conditioned to hate flowers and books. Books and roses are displayed in a way that make them irresistably attractive to the babies. Following their natural instinct, the infants are eager to touch the objects. Just as they reach out to get them, there is an explosion, the sound of alarm-bells, and they even receive an electric shock. According to the Behaviourist theory, after about 200 repetitions, the babies unconsciously link the attractiveness of books and roses with their fear of noise and electric shocks, and are thus efficiently taught to keep away from the objects they once desired. Before we're going to talk about the psychological theory that is at the basis of this experiment, we'll start by explaining the name of the rooms:

Ivan Pavlov (1849–1936) was a famous Russian physiologist and has sometimes been called the "father of Behaviourism". By means of experiments he tried to establish his theory of the "conditioned reflex". The most important experiment that is popularly linked with his name is the so-called "Pavlovian Dog" experiment. When a dog sees or smells food, its normal reaction to it will be salivation (food = native or unconditioned stimulus). Pavlov showed that if a bell is rung every time the food is presented, eventually the bell alone will be enough to cause a salivary response. The bell will have become a "substitute stimulus". The importance of Pavlov's experiment lies in the fact that one can deliberately widen the range of stimuli and still get the same reaction.

A closer look at the theory of Behaviourism and its importance as a psychological theory will easily show us the connection between Pavlov's experiments and the use that the BN Worlders make of Behaviourism.

Some information on Behaviourism

The origin of Behaviourism as a psychological theory goes back to the year 1912, when John B. Watson daringly started to apply to the study of man the same research methods that had for years only been used to describe animal behaviour. (See also Pavlov's experiments.) It had so far been agreed that human consciousness was the main point of interest in psychology. The behaviourist however, as is suggested by his very name, is convinced that human behaviour, 'What the organism does or says' (p. 6), must be made the only object of research. Needless to say that this new approach to the problems of psychology provoked contradictory reactions. Its critics doubted that one could analyze the complexity of a human being merely by describing and conditioning its reactions to certain 'stimuli'. A further, and perhaps more important, point of criticism is the fear of manipulation. As soon as one is able to train ("condition") people's reactions, one controls them; one is able to form or change their personalities according to one's own convenience. Even though the behaviourists themselves have never left any doubts about their intentions being entirely positive and beneficial to mankind, Huxley's description of the behaviourist experiment must be seen as a satirical warning against the dangers of manipulation and dispossessed consciousness.

Unterrichtsschritt 3:
Text on Behaviourism

In the text we're made familiar with the basic terms of behaviourism: "stimulus" and "response". It stands to reason that, within the given frame of thought, human behaviour can be defined as a series of responses to certain stimuli. What is important though, is the fact that stimuli as well as responses can be changed or "conditioned". The experiment in the "Neo-Pavlovian Conditioning Rooms" is an example of "conditioned response". The babies' first response to the sight of books and flowers is delight. As soon as these objects have become indissolubly wedded with the disagreeable sensation of electric shocks and loud noise, the same objects will cause fear and horror:

Stimulus: *Response:*
Sight of roses ——————→ Delight
and books

Stimulus: *Response:*
Electric shocks, noise ————→ Fear

Stimulus: *Conditoned Response:*
Roses, books ——————→ Fear, Flight

J. B. Watson "Behaviorism"

The Behaviorist's Platform

The behaviorist asks: Why don't we make what we can *observe* the real field of psychology? Let us limit ourselves to things that can be observed, and formulate laws concerning only those things. Now what can we observe? We can observe *behavior – what the organism does or says.*

The rule, or measuring rod, which the behaviorist puts in front of him always is: Can I describe this bit of behavior I see in terms of "stimulus and response"?

General Nature Of Psychological Problems And Solutions

Let us use the abbreviations S for *stimulus* (or the more complex *situation*) and R for *response.* We may schematise our psychological problems as follows:

S . . . . R
Given   ? (to be determined)

S . . . . R
? (to be determined)   given

Your problem reaches its explanation always when:

S . . . . R
has been determined   has been determined

Suppose for example we take an already established reaction
with both stimulus and response known, such as:
S . . . . R
Electric shock   Withdrawal of hand

Now the mere visual stimulus of a patch of red light will not cause the withdrawal of the hand. The patch of red light may produce no marked reaction whatsoever (what reaction does appear will depend upon previous conditioning). But if I show the red light and then immediately or shortly thereafter stimulate my subject's hand with the electric current and repeat this routine often enough, the red light will cause the immediate withdrawal of the hand. The red light now becomes a substitute stimulus – it will call out the R whenever it stimulates the subject in that setting. Something has happened to bring about this change. This change, as we have pointed out, is called conditioning – the reaction remains the same but we have increased the number of stimuli that will call it out. To express the new state of affairs we (rather inaccurately) describe the change by speaking of the *stimulus* as being *"conditioned".*

Substitution of Response

Can we substitute or condition responses? Experiment teaches us that the process of response substitution or conditioning does take place in all animals throughout life. Yesterday his puppy called out from a two-year-old child – fondling, pet words, play and laughter:

S .... R
Sight of dog   Manipulation, laughter.

Today the same dog calls out:

S .... R
Sight of dog   Screaming, withdrawal of body.

Something happened. Late yesterday the dog bit him too hard in play – broke the skin and caused bleeding. We know that

S .... R
Cutting, burning of skin   withdrawal of body, screaming.

In other words while the visual stimulus *dog* has remained substantially the same, the reaction belonging to another unconditioned stimulus (cutting, pricking skin) has made its appearance.[1]

John B. Watson, Behaviorism, New York 1970 (Norton) (First published: 1924)

Questions:
1) What according to Behaviourists, does human behaviour consist of?
2) What's the Behaviourist's field of research?
3) What is a "conditioned stimulus" and what is a "conditioned response"?
4) What's the experiment in the "Neo-Pavlovian Conditioning Rooms" an example of?

Unterrichtschritt 4:
B. F. Skinner, "Walden Two"

B. F. Skinner (born 1904) is considered to be one of the leading representatives of behaviourist psychology and one of the founding fathers of programmed learning.
In his first and only novel "Walden Two" (1948, cf. Reference books), he describes the utopian model of a society: a group of some hundred people live together without any aggressions and with a minimum of restraint. Things like inequality, competition, dependence, suppression and power don't exist any more. The members of this society have – according to the behaviourist theory – been conditioned to "always do what they want, what they choose to do", but the general managers ensure that "they want to do what is good for them and the society they live in". One of the most interesting aspects of this kind of society is childrearing and education.

It presents certain parallels with "BNW". Babies are, however, born in a natural way by mothers who are normally about 18 years old. Just like in "BNW", the traditional family doesn't exist any more: the babies aren't brought up by their parents, they grow up together in a kind of children's hotel. Instead of the love of their mother and father, they experience the love of the whole community. The behaviourist method of reinforcement and reward together with phases of ethical training are the leading principles of education in Skinner's utopian society.

The non-existence of the traditional family should at this point not perhaps be discussed at length, but it might be worth while discussing the educational principles of the Behaviourists in general, and particularly the methods applied in "Walden Two".

Unterrichtsschritt 5:
Hypnopaedia
and Neo-Pavlovian conditioning

We can summarize the aim of Pavlovian conditioning in BNW by saying that it is supposed to programme people's reactions to certain things and circumstances. The meaning of the word "reaction" here being: nonverbalized and preconscious behaviour. But, as the D.H.C. rightly says: "wordless conditioning is crude and wholesale", because your thinking can only be conditioned by words. Childishly simple sentences are repeated 40–50 times a night. The structure of the sentences, their suggestive exaggeration ("frightfully clever, awfully glad") remind us of some of the simpler slogans in advertising.

Hypnopaedia (sleep-teaching) had only just been rediscovered when Huxley wrote his novel. The method as such, i.e. making use of people's sleep in order to suggest certain ideas, goes back to Ancient Greece (Greek temple sleep). In "BNW Revisited" Huxley mentions some further studies in the field of hypnopaedia. In the "Psychological Bulletin for July 1955" (p. 125) scientists tried to find out whether people could be taught during their sleep; some experiments during the Second World War, all kinds of auto-suggestions, and another experiment described in the "Journal of Clinical and Experimental Hypnosis for October 1956" (p. 127) seem to prove that light sleep is a state in which many subjects will accept suggestions as readily as they do when under hypnosis (p. 128). As a teaching method, hypnopaedia has never actually been made use of, because psychologists soon realized that it could inhibit the development of the child's personality. Some forms of psychological training, like hypnotherapy and self-administered suggestion, do, however, bear a certain resemblance to it.

Does that mean that Huxley's horrible picture of a child's (and thus an adult's) mind being nothing but a pile of suggestions has not come true and will never be likely to? What Huxley is concerned about, is not so much the method, but its result: manipulation of suggestion-prone human beings. "Is individual freedom compatible with a high degree of individual suggestibility?" (p. 133)

Sequenz 3: Brave New World's Ideology

5./6. Stunde:
The New Gods

Zur didaktischen Funktion

Das dritte Kapitel, anhand dessen die ideologischen Prämissen der Schönen Neuen Welt besonders gut dargestellt und nachvollzogen werden können, hat eine komplexe Struktur. Es scheint daher unerläßlich, gemeinsam mit den Schülern die verschiedenen Elemente (Ort, Zeit, Personen) und ihre jeweilige Funktion herauszuarbeiten. Erst im Anschluß an diese Analyse sollte man sich dem Herausarbeiten der ideologischen Inhalte zuwenden.

Ausgangspunkt einer Analyse der verschiedenen Ideologien sollte die Gestalt des „zweieinigen" Gottes ‚Ford/Freud' sein, in deren Namen die totale Manipulation der Menschen vor sich geht. Die Einstellung der Brave New Worlder zu allen zentralen Lebensfragen (Ethik, Religion, Tod, Wissenschaft usw.) erklärt sich auf dem Hintergrund Freudscher und Fordscher Theorien und Lehren bzw. ihrer Weiterentwicklung und Verfälschung.

Es ist demnach sinnvoll, die Schüler über gewisse Teile der Freudschen Theorie, vor allem seine Ausführungen über frühkindliche Sexualität und deren Einflüsse auf die Persönlichkeitsentwicklung, zu informieren. Von daher wird auch deutlich, wie das System Freuds Erkenntnisse in seinen Dienst nimmt, verfälscht und als Unterdrückungsinstrument einsetzt.

Die Rolle, die Ford in BNW spielt, ist weniger vermittelt und kann durch Aktivierung der Vorkenntnisse der Schüler oder durch gesteuerte Lehrerfragen leicht festgehalten werden.

Ziele der Stunde

Die Schüler sollen
— die Struktur des Kapitels 3 als symbolische Darstellung des Kontrasts zwischen "BNW" und der alten (also unserer) Welt erkennen
— sich darüber klar werden, welche Assoziationen der Name „Ford" evoziert
— wissen, wer Freud war und welche Bedeutung er hatte
— durch den Zusatztext erfahren, auf welchen Teil der Freudschen Theorie Huxley Bezug nimmt
— (durch den Schülervortrag über die Sage von Ödipus informiert werden)

Verlaufsskizze

Voraussetzungen:
Kapitel 3 ist gründlich gelesen, und die Schüler sind in der Lage, es zusammenzufassen.

Unterrichtsschritt 1:

Die komplexe Struktur des dritten Kapitels wird anhand von Leitfragen analysiert.

Unterrichtsschritt 2:

a) Die Schüler werden aufgefordert, zu überlegen, was ihnen zu dem Namen „Ford" einfällt, und notieren ihre Gedanken in Stichworten. (Eine Hilfe könnte vom Lehrer evtl. noch durch Dias gegeben werden: Hochhäuser, Fabriken, Fließbandarbeit, Maschinen, Verkehrschaos etc.)

b) Die Ergebnisse werden systematisiert und an der Tafel festgehalten.

Unterrichtsschritt 3:

Kurzer Lehrervortrag darüber, in welcher Form Freuds Theorien in den Roman eingegangen sind.

Unterrichtsschritt 4:

a) Den ausgeteilten Text über Freud bearbeiten die Schüler gruppenweise.
b) Das Ergebnis der Gruppenarbeit wird an der Tafel festgehalten. (Siehe T. A.)

Unterrichtsschritt 5:

Ein Schüler hat den Auftrag erhalten, mit einigen Sätzen seine Mitschüler über den antiken Ödipus-Mythos zu informieren. Diese Phase kann bei entsprechendem Vorwissen der Schüler auch entfallen.

Zusätzliche Diskussionspunkte

– *Zu Unterrichtsschritt 2:* Massenproduktion, Konsumgesellschaft, Verschleiß, die „Fordschen Segnungen".
– *Zu Unterrichtsschritt 3 + 4:* Ist der Angriff gerechtfertigt? (Mögliche Alternativen)

Zum Inhalt der Stunde

Unterrichtsschritt 1:
The structure of the third chapter

In the third chapter the old and the new worlds are opposed. This is done by skilfully blending different levels of action: the DHC (Director of the Hatchery) and the students are watching the children's erotic play in the garden; Henry Foster, the Assistant Predestinator and Bernard Marx meet in the lift at the end of their shift; Lenina and Fanny Crowne are having a conversation in the Girls' Dressing Room; Mustapha Mond, the world controller has meanwhile joined the students in the garden and is telling them about the bad old days; and in the nurseries we can hear the whispering voices of the sleep-teachers. The antagonism between the old and the new world is satirically presented at all the different levels: the children playing erotic games and the over-adjusted students listening to Mustapha Mond's stories about the old world and neurotic people living in squalid and overcrowded homes. Then there is Henry Foster's and the Predestinator's conversation about girls, bitterly commented on by Bernard's (unuttered) thoughts and his unorthodox feelings. In the female world of wonderful smells and sterile cleanliness, Lenina and Fanny are having a shower, while they're casually talking about promiscuity and "Pregnancy Substitutes". Even though Lenina shows streaks of consciousness and doubt, the two girls are perfectly well adapted to BNW's psychological principles, and the whispering voices of the nurseries illustrate ironically *what* kind of principles the Brave New Worlders have got to conform to.

The structure of this chapter clearly shows us the ironical parallel and the incompatibility of a "squalid" old and a "brave" new world, and we're naturally led to ask ourselves what the ideological background of such a world is like.

Unterrichtsschritt 2:
Our Ford, the new God

Even before the world controller explicitly introduces Ford-(Freud) as BNW's God, we've heard the DHC speaking of "Our Ford", and we know that the Christian era has come to an end. (It's not anno Domini

A.D., but anno Fordi A.F.). The striking phonetic resemblance between "Ford" and "Lord", however, might have induced us to read over it, without giving it any further thought. (See also: Fordship-Lordship).

The symbol of Ford is a T, derived from his Model car T (see also further down), but which might also be interpreted as a mutilation of the Christian cross. The Christian cross has been 'beheaded' in every sense of the word.

What kind of God is Ford, then?

The real Henry Ford (1863–1947) started his career as an engineer, and later became one of the world's most important industrialists. As early as 1892 he built his first car, and in 1903 he founded the Ford Motor Company. But only the production of his famous 'Model T' (1908) established Ford's world-wide reputation. More than 15 million of these cars were sold between 1908 and 1927. This was the beginning of mass production. In 1913 Ford installed moving assembly lines that turned out in 93 minutes what had before taken 14 hours. Ford's economic and social principles (also sometimes called "Fordism") are based on the idea that a mass production system, implying division of labour and rationalizations cuts costs and makes lower market prices possible. Ford's books "My Life and Work" (1922) and "To-day and To-morrow" (1926) contributed to the legend of Henry Ford and made him one of the founding fathers of modern industrialized society. The pupils might not know all the details about Ford, but they're certainly aware of his importance, and their associations will unmistakably evoke the picture of a modern industrial society of mass production and consumption, money, cars, speed, mad activity etc. ("...ending is better than mending... I love new clothes... etc.", p. 64) and suggest Huxley's appalling vision of "identical twins... working identical machines" (p. 23). Ford's notorious joke about the first mass-product, his Model T: "They can have any

colour they like, provided it's black" can, in BNW, satirically be applied to another mass-product, man: "They can have any individually they like, provided they're identical."

Unterrichtsschritt 3:
Our Freud:

Freud's studies of family relationships and his concepts concerning the conditions of culture make a large contribution to BNW's ideology. The attempt to trace his theory throughout the book, and to point out the Brave New Worlders distortions of his values, would take us too far. What we'll do is just pick out three situations, where Freud's ideas have come to serve BNW's purposes:

(1) At the beginning of the third chapter, several hundred little boys and girls are playing erotic games. This kind of "sexual education" is based on one of Sigmund Freud's (1856–1939) most important findings. In his "Essays on the Theory of Sexuality", Freud deals, among other things, with infantile sexuality. He says: "Sexual life does not begin only at puberty, but starts with plain manifestations soon after birth" (p. 89). As a consequence he then mentions what Mustapha Mond presented as "the appalling dangers of family life", i.e. the parents' repression of the child's sexual pleasure, inhibition and the risk of causing neuroses. In BNW the children freely indulge in infantile eroticism, which is considered an important step in the process of preparing them for promiscuity and sexual licence.

(2) When Mustapha Mond says: "Our Freud had been the first to reveal the appalling dangers of family life", he mainly refers to the fact that BNW has completely abolished the "dangerous" relationship between parents and children. No mothers, no fathers, brothers or sisters, no families that could cause "perversion, madness and suicide" (p. 52). It must be their own idea of Freud's well-known theory of the so-called "Oedipus complex"

Freud believed that since the child's first intimate human relationship is normally with the mother, or someone who fulfils her role in his nursing and upbringing, she will always be the child's first love. He coined two phrases to define exactly what he meant about this aspect of the development of sexuality in the human race. Sexual objects are the people or things to whom we direct the libido, our internal drive towards sexual gratification. The channelling of this drive he called sexual aim.

But even in infancy the secret passion of the child for the mother cannot remain either innocent in the child's own mind or capable of fulfilment with any degree of completeness. It cannot be fulfilled because the child cannot have the mother entirely to himself; it cannot remain innocent because the child links the obvious parental disapproval of his sexual excitement with his own secret feelings of jealousy and competitiveness towards his father, whom he inevitably and intuitively perceives as a rival for the mother's affection, attention and all else which he wants from her, and which she is in some way able to give also to his father.

To this situation Freud gave the name of the Oedipus complex, based upon the classic Greek myth of the innocent prince of Thebes who the oracle predicts will murder his father and marry his mother.

The Oedipus complex has to be conceived as the child's real but repressed fear that the father will castrate him in retaliation for the desire for exclusive possession of the mother. In attempting to describe this complex in words, we are of course using the words in a way in which no subject of such a complex ever could. No infant could formulate the Oedipus complex in words, nor indeed could an infant confide, explain, confess or even request reassurance in words. Yet feelings as deeply charged as these cannot be endured consciously and so are repressed. With the repression of the Oedipus complex, the period of infantile sexual activity and conscious excitement comes to an end. Sexual feelings remain, but they are diminished and all too often disowned. Curiosity persists, but there are very few children who dare ask questions. The period between about five and about eleven during which this deceptive calm appears to reign, was called by Freud the latency period.

David Stafford-Clark, What Freud Really Said, Penguin Books, 1967

1) Why can the child's secret passion for the mother not remain innocent?
2) Where is the name "Oedipus complex" derived from?
3) What is the result of the child's fear of his father?
4) What did Freud call the "latency period"?
5) Why is Freud BNW's "second" God? What use have they made of his theories?

that causes the Brave New Worlder's ridiculous horror of the relationship between mother and son.
(3) The third allusion to Freud's ideas is less obvious, but is implicit in Mond's attitude towards "high art" and creativity. Let's however put off the analysis of what Freud meant by his term "sublimation" until we have had a closer look at the dispute about "high art" and "happiness" in lesson 13.

Unterrichtsschritt 4:
The Oedipus complex

The additional text (cf. p. 31) will give the pupils an idea of this popularly known concept of the "Oedipus complex" and will so enable them see what the Brave New Worlders have come to make of it.

7. Stunde:
"History is Bunk"

Zur didaktischen Funktion

Nachdem man in der vorausgegangenen Doppelstunde auf die Bedeutung von Ford und Freud eingegangen ist, soll nun gezeigt werden, weshalb Geschichte im System von Brave New World keinen Platz haben kann. Ford und Freud stehen als historische Figuren nur scheinbar im Widerspruch zu dieser Geschichtslosigkeit. Geschichte bedeutet Entwicklung, Veränderung, Kritik und Bewegung; jegliche Art von Veränderung aber ist mit der statischen neuen Welt unvereinbar. Ford und Freud dürfen in BNW nicht in ihrer geschichtlichen Rolle als Neuerer gesehen werden, sondern als Galionsfiguren eines festgefügten Systems, das sorgfältig darauf bedacht ist, Erschütterungen zu vermeiden. Zum Abschluß dieser Unterrichtsstunde soll noch einmal zusammengefaßt werden, welche Entwicklungstendenzen der zwanziger und dreißiger Jahre Huxley in seiner Satire aufs Korn genommen hat.

Ziele der Stunde

Die Schüler sollen
– erkennen, was der Begriff „Geschichte" beinhaltet und weshalb er mit der Forderung nach sozialer Stabilität unvereinbar ist

– zusammenfassen können, welche Tendenzen der zwanziger und dreißiger Jahre Huxley in seiner Satire dargestellt hat.

Verlaufsskizze

Voraussetzungen:
siehe vorige Stunde

Unterrichtsschritt 1:

Der Abschnitt über Geschichte (S. 48, "You all remember…" bis S. 49, "…overwhelmed with confusion.") wird laut gelesen und vom Lehrer kurz erläutert.

Unterrichtsschritt 2:

Im Unterrichtsgespräch wird ermittelt, warum Geschichte und soziale Stabilität unvereinbar sind. (T. A. hierzu erst nach Unterrichtsschritt 3).

Unterrichtsschritt 3:

a) Kurzes feed-back zum Begriff "happiness" (siehe 2. Stunde)
b) In *Stillarbeit* lesen die Schüler von S. 178, "A new Theory of Biology" …bis S. 179 "…if one didn't have to think about happiness." und beantworten die Frage nach dem Glücksbegriff (siehe Stundenblatt) in Stichworten (evtl. graphische Skizze)
c) Das Ergebnis des Unterrichtsgesprächs (U 2) und der Stillarbeit wird an der Tafel festgehalten.

Unterrichtsschritt 4:

Auf Folie werden noch einmal einige Grundprinzipien von Huxleys neuer Gesellschaft festgehalten (z. B. consumerism, genetic manipulation etc.), und die Schüler versuchen, die entsprechenden – von Huxley satirisch überzeichneten – Tendenzen der zwanziger und dreißiger Jahre zu ergänzen.

Zusätzliche Diskussionspunkte

– *Zu Unterrichtsschritt 2 + 3:* Geschichte und Geschichtsdarstellung in totalitären Regimen. (Interessant wäre vor allem ein Vergleich mit Orwells „1984“)

Inhalt der Stunde:

Unterrichtsschritt 1:
Mond's examples of history

Mustapha Mond himself gives us an idea of what history means, when he mentions the names of peoples, Gods, Kings and writers. Mond speaks of "Harappa", the remnants of a prehistoric Indian town in West Pakistan that had been excavated in the 19th century, "Ur of the Chaldees", another famous prehistoric town, going back to the year 2500 B. C., he mentions Thebes and Babylon, names of prehistoric cultures, Gods (Jupiter, Gotama, Jesus), kingdoms, myths, writers (Shakespeare, Pascal) and works of art.

Unterrichtsschritt 2 + 3:
"History is bunk"

Although this saying is not Huxley's invention and has actually always been ascribed to Henry Ford, Mustapha Mond applies it to BNW in a deeper and more philosophical sense than Ford could ever have conceived. In a broader sense "history" could mean anything that happened during and before the existence of the earth, thus including natural history. But history in Mond's sense, the history that has been banned from BNW, is the history of man. Examples that show us that man is neither eternal nor perfect, that he's capable of great cultural achievements and powerful ideas that will all decay and perhaps leave nothing but "specks of antique dirt" that must be "brushed away". History means constant change: progress, decay, improvement, deterioration, success and failure. Once we accept this "definition" of history it becomes evident that any attempt to pin down man's behaviour and lay down rules for the future development of mankind becomes difficult, if not altogether impossible. Mustapha Mond is clearly aware of this. His World State is based on social stability, and social stability can only be achieved if every single individual is calculable, manageable, unchangeable, and – in his own way – perfect. History has become useless, "bunk" in the truest sense of the word, because the future will be the same as the present, and the present has never been different from what it is now. Eternal present means stagnation, immutability and restriction, but, at the same time, it means stability, security and tranquillity, it means everything that the word "social stability" implies for the Brave New Worlders, and Mustapha Mond knows that, once more, he must sacrifice the "enlargement of knowledge", the "intensification and refining of consciousness" (p. 179), for the sake of BNW's "Sovereign Good", "happiness" and "social stability".

Unterrichtsschritt 4:
Huxley's main targets of satire

After talking about BNW's human production and its ideology, we can already try to summarize Huxley's main targets of satire. In his novel, the author presents the picture of a society that has turned all our values upside down. Any kind of suspicious tendency that a close observer might have noticed in the twenties and thirties of our century has been perverted and distorted:

1) Ford's – admittedly dangerous – ideas about mass-production have been turned into an absurd form of conditioned consumerism ("I do love flying" / "I do love

having new clothes" / "Old clothes are beastly" etc.) that even affects the Brave New Worlder's relationship to nature: "A love of nature keeps no factories busy". (p. 37).

2) The principle of mass-production and new findings in the field of genetics have been combined to enable the mass-production of test-tube babies (humans) whose outward health and eternal youth can merely be interpreted as a sign of their psychic and emotional disease.

3) The possibilities of the behavioristic concept have become a powerful instrument of manipulation, alienation and complete adaptation.

4) Some people's hope for social justice and equal chances (Marxist and Socialist ideas) have been merged into an absurd concept of "identity" and a rigid caste system that prohibits any kind of social mobility.

5) Modern industrial society with its machines, its means of transport and communication has been transformed into a sterile world, where man himself has become an interchangeable spare part of a huge machine.

6) Mustapha Mond, the intelligent, eloquent World-Controller reminds us of the managers in charge of H. G. Well's world state, and he could even be considered as a satirical counterpart to the philosopher King of Plato's "Politeia".

Um den inhaltlichen Zusammenhang besser zu wahren, wäre es freilich möglich – wenn auch nicht unbedingt notwendig – die zu diesem Zweck „ausgelassenen" Kapitel kurz zusammenzufassen.

Die hier behandelten Kapitel zeigen einen weiteren Aspekt des ideologischen Überbaus dieses Gesellschaftssystems: die Einstellung der Brave New Worlder zum Tod, zu Religion und zu ethischen Fragen im weiteren Sinne.

Nicht nur in Huxleys schöner neuer Welt, auch in unserer hochindustrialisierten Gesellschaft, läßt die Einstellung zum Tod weitreichende Schlüsse zu. Was Evelyn Waugh in seinem Buch „Tod in Hollywood" ("The Loved One") zeigt, nämlich die Unfähigkeit, die eigene Sterblichkeit mit Würde zu ertragen, würde in BNW ins Groteske übersteigert. Es sollte im Verlauf dieser Unterrichtseinheit klar werden, daß die Einstellung der Brave New Worlder zum Tod gar nicht anders sein kann. Jeder einzelne dieser synthetischen Massenmenschen ist ersetzbar und kann ohne Verlust ausgetauscht werden. Es besteht keine Bindung der Menschen untereinander, und deshalb ist der Tod eines Individuums ebenso nebensächlich wie die Frage nach dem Sinn seines Lebens und dem Menschen selbst. Diese Sicht des Todes und das dazugehörige Menschenbild liegt Mustapha Monds Ausführungen über Religion und Ethik zugrunde und führt ihn zu dem logischen Schluß, daß die schöne neue Welt weder das eine noch das andere braucht.

8. Stunde:
Death, Religion, and Ethics

Zur didaktischen Funktion

Da die Unterrichtseinheit nach thematischen Schwerpunkten hin konzipiert ist, muß in dieser Stunde ein Sprung vom dritten zum 14. bzw. 17. Kapitel gemacht werden.

Ziele der Stunde

Die Schüler sollen
– erkennen, welche Rolle das Phänomen „Tod" in BNW spielt, und mit welchen Mitteln der Autor diese Rolle deutlich macht
– durch das Referat über Waughs „Tod in

Hollywood" ähnliche Tendenzen in unserer Gesellschaft wahrnehmen
– sich darüber klar werden, welcher Zusammenhang zwischen der Einstellung gegenüber dem Tod und der allgemein herrschenden Ethik besteht.

Verlaufsskizze

Voraussetzungen

a) Das Kapitel 14 (ganz) und das Gespräch zwischen Mond und John Kapitel 17 (vor allem Seiten 228–235) wurde von allen Schülern gründlich gelesen.
b) Ein Schüler hat ein Referat über E. Waughs „Tod in Hollywood" vorbereitet.
c) Zwei Schüler haben das Gespräch S. 228–235 als "debate" vorbereitet, wobei einer die Argumente Monds, ein weiterer die Johns übernimmt.

Unterrichtsschritt 1:

Im Unterrichtsgespräch soll herausgearbeitet werden, welche Atmosphäre in dem Moribundenhospital herrscht und wie sich daraus die Einstellung der Brave New Worlder zum Tod ableiten läßt.
Die Ergebnisse des Gesprächs werden an der Tafel festgehalten (siehe T. A.).

Unterrichtsschritt 2:

Das Schülerreferat über Waughs „Tod in Hollywood" informiert die Schüler über Todesrituale in einer modernen Industriegesellschaft.

Unterrichtsschritt 3:

In Form einer (vorbereiteten) "debate" geben zwei Schüler das Gespräch (S. 228–235) zwischen Mustapha Mond und John wieder.

Unterrichtsschritt 4:

Diese "debate" wird gemeinsam zusammengefaßt und das Ergebnis an der Tafel festgehalten.

Zum Inhalt der Stunde

Unterrichtsschritt 1:
The insignificance of death

It seems a strange confusion: a description that might have been applied to the Hatchery: "bright sunshine... yellow paint... gay melodies... a thoroughly pleasant atmosphere (p. 198) is what we find in Park Lane Hospital for the Dying". There's nothing like "wintriness, frozen light" or "pallid shapes" (p. 19). Birth in BNW seems to evoke rather unpleasant feelings, whereas death is connected with sunshine, brightness, pleasant melodies and perfumes. Nothing is irrational in BNW, so the confusion must be explicable. The birth of a Brave New Worlder is nothing anybody is particularly happy about or interested in. There's no family, no friends who could welcome the new-born baby. Birth is nothing but the making and finishing of a mass product that can be infinitely reproduced. No need, then, to create a pleasant atmosphere in a place that is nothing but a factory producing human beings.

Death, on the other hand, is a phenomenon that, in itself, is not particularly pleasant either, but it is something that should go unnoticed and without fuss. It's like throwing away a broken cog-wheel that has to be replaced as quickly as possible, so that the functioning of the system is not interrupted. Just as any spare-part is unaware of being replaced, the Brave New Worlders are unaware of their passing away, and if, despite the progress of science, any unpleasant feelings or sensations should occur, there's always *Soma* and a "pleasant atmosphere" that keep people ignorant of what is really going on.

As love, friendship and family are unknown in BNW, nobody can be missed, nobody is wept for, there is no mourning. John's visit to Park Lane Hospital is one of the few occasions where the reader is able to completely identify with John. To our way of thinking, his behaviour is normal and adequate. The nurse's innocent small-talk, her surprise, her blunt statement of the situation ("No, of course there isn't", p. 198) seems strangely incongruous and irreverent. Just like John, the reader can hardly believe that even deeply-rooted feelings like awe and helplessness can be manipulated and maimed. There's no chance of communication between the two worlds, and, together with John, the reader can only "shudder as he looks" (p. 199) at this disparity between outward youth and inward decay.

Unterrichtsschritt 2:
Evelyn Waugh, "The Loved One"

Evelyn Waugh (1903–1966) was an English novelist who wrote several witty, ironical novels about the English upper-class. In his novel "The Loved One", however, he satirizes American (Californian) funeral customs. Through the eyes of an ironical unsuccessful English poet, he describes the embalming-rooms, the crematoria and the ludicrous dignity of the funeral institute of 'Whispering Glades'.

Unterrichtsschritt 3 + 4:
Death, old age and ethics

Death and old age cannot be considered separately, so what has been described in chapter 14, must necessarily be compared to what Mond says about old age in chapter 17 (pp. 230/31 pp. 233–35). Old age, according to Mond, is the loss of everything that makes life worth while, i.e. beauty, youth, prosperity, activity and pleasant sensations. It's the fear of losing these things, more than the fear

of Death itself, that makes old people "turn to religion". If, as in BNW, people are endowed with eternal youth, they remain active and dynamic to the very end of their days; they don't see the necessity of "hunting for a substitute". Since they have been conditioned to be happy members of a society that goes in for superficial pleasures, to accept life as it is, and not to think about its deeper sense, they have consequently *not* been "conditioned to believe in God" (p. 232). Mond's conclusions are consistent, and John is hardly given a chance to get in his counter-arguments. It's the very consistency of BNW's system that makes it so difficult to attack, even if we're clearly aware of its horrors and fundamental errors. John's attack mainly consists of questions that show his utter confusion ("But isn't it natural to feel there is a God..." / "But all the same it is natural to believe in God", p. 232 / "Doesn't there seem to be a God?" / ..."Are you sure?" p. 233) and that allow Mond to set things right and show him that the world has changed, and that his Christian ethics have become obsolete and superfluous: "God isn't compatible with machinery" (p. 232) and "There isn't any need for a civilized man to bear anything that's seriously unpleasant" (p. 234).

9. Stunde:
The Role of Science

Zur didaktischen Funktion

Freiheit, Gleichheit, Tod, Ethik, Gott – all diese Begriffe haben in BNW ihre ursprüngliche Bedeutung eingebüßt und sind zu bloßen Worthülsen geworden, haben sich in ihr Gegenteil verkehrt. Es sollte den Schülern in dieser Stunde klargemacht werden, daß die Begriffsverwirrung auch vor der Wissenschaft nicht haltmacht. BNW ist eine hochtechnisierte, sich aufgeklärt dünkende Gesellschaft, die all ihre Errungenschaften der Wissenschaft verdankt. Man sollte demnach annehmen, daß zumindest der Wissenschaft der ihr gebührende Platz eingeräumt wird, daß – moralische Skrupel bestehen ja nicht mehr – ungehindert geforscht und experimentiert werden kann. Zunächst wird man also erstaunt sein, den Äußerungen Monds zu entnehmen, daß auch die Wissenschaft „auf Eis gelegt wurde", daß ihr Sinn und Ziel, *Neues,* zu entdecken und anzuwenden, unerwünscht ist. Doch bei näherem Hinsehen ergänzt gerade diese Erkenntnis den Teufelskreis der Begriffsverwirrung und weist wieder auf das hin, was den Weltstaat zusammenhält: die soziale Stabilität.

Bei der Gegenüberstellung der zwei Wissenschaftsbegriffe (freie und „zensierte" Wissenschaft), sollte man auf keinen Fall versäumen, auf das ethische Problem der Verantwortlichkeit des Wissenschaftlers näher einzugehen. Denn gerade im Bereich der Genetik (siehe Einleitung) und der Physik stellt sich auch in unserer Gesellschaft die Frage, ob auf jedem Gebiet bedenkenlos und uneingeschränkt geforscht werden sollte.

Ziele der Stunde

Die Schüler sollen
– in der Lage sein, „richtige" Wissenschaft und Wissenschaft, wie sie in BNW betrieben wird, gegeneinander abzugrenzen
– erkennen, daß auch das Wort „Wissenschaft" dem sprachlichen Verwirrspiel der Neuen Welt zum Opfer gefallen ist
– sich – durch Zitate angeregt – Gedanken über die Verantwortlichkeit des Wissenschaftlers machen

Verlaufsskizze

Voraussetzungen:

Kapitel 16 (insbesondere S. 223, "Science…" bis S. 226, "…I paid too.") wurde gründlich gelesen. Die Schüler haben zu Hause versucht, aufzuschreiben, was man untere dem Begriff „Wissenschaft" versteht.

Unterrichtsschritt 1:

In Form eines Unterrichtsgesprächs wird die Hausaufgabe (Begriffsdefinition + Inhalt von Kapitel 16) besprochen. Das Ziel dieses Unterrichtsgesprächs ist ein Vergleich zwischen Wissenschaft, wie sie in BNW betrieben wird, und „richtiger" Wissenschaft.

Unterrichtsschritt 2:

Den Schülern werden in Form einer Hektographie (vgl. S. 39) einzelne Sätze aus Aufsätzen und ähnlichen Quellen vorgelegt, die eine Diskussion über die Verantwortlichkeit des Wissenschaftlers anregen sollen.

Zum Inhalt der Stunde

Zu Unterrichtsschritt 1:
The role of science

"Science may be defined as the reduction of multiplicity to unity." (BNW Revisited, p. 36). This is Huxley's definition of science in "BNW Revisited". And he explains his definition by pointing out the difference between the non-scientific way of seeing things separately as one unique entity ("an apple is an apple is an apple…", p. 37) and the scientific method of combining things by means of a certain theory (Newton's theory of gravitation).
Science is based on observation. The scientist carefully observes the different steps in a pro-

cess (usually this process is the result of an experiment). When he has collected all the observations, he tries to explain the phenomenon, i.e. to find out what occurs regularly, allowing him to form a so-called hypothesis. The next experiments are done to see whether his hypothesis is right or wrong. Should it prove wrong, it will be rejected; if it proves to be right, it will, by means of further experiments, become a scientific theory. So what are the qualities required of a scientist? They are: meticulous and laborious research, an objectivity that excludes any kind of bias, prejudice or suspicion, an open-mindedness towards new ways of thinking, and, last but not least, a certain creativeness and courage that prevent the scientist from simply treading a given path.

But what has science become in BNW? John doesn't know very much about it, but he's right when he says that science is "something you made helicopters with, ... something that prevented you from being wrinkled and losing your teeth..." (p. 223). It certainly is the basis of technology and medicine, it is what makes people laugh at suspicious rituals; but not even Helmholtz understands Mond, when he says that "Science is dangerous", that is has to be kept "chained and muzzled". What science is, or can be, is determined by its aim.

The aim of science is generally considered to be progress, improvement, greater knowledge and change (for the better?!). We know by now that BNW's foremost aim is social stability, and so the hypnopaedic platitude that "Science is everything" must be reconsidered in that light. If science were left to develop freely, this would necessarily imply that its present stage is only transitory, and that every new experiment is liable to open new prospects. The slogan "Science is everything" means that even though BNW owes all its technological and biological achievements to science, science has lost its right to existence, as soon as it has help the BNWorlders to reach their ultimate aim of social stability. Science that is "carefully chained and muzzled". Science that is not allowed to make any new discoveries whatsoever, that is like a "cookery book with an orthodox theory of cooking that nobody is allowed to question..." (p. 224), is no science at all and has kept its name merely for the sake of deferential gratitude towards the good work it had done in the past, i.e. establishing in BNW "the stablest equilibrium in history".

Unterrichtsschritt 2:
Controlling scientific progress?

So Brave New World's reasons for controlling scientific progress are pretty obvious and simple: it's "happiness rather than truth and beauty" (p. 226) that matters.

And what about our world today? Don't we agree with Mond when he asks what the "point of truth or beauty or knowledge" is, "when anthrax bombs are popping all around you" (p. 226). It's certainly a different kind of happiness that we long for, when we think of controlling scientific progress. Our happiness should be the result of an ethical sense of responsibility, that might spare us anthrax bombs as well as Bokanovsky Groups and Neo-Pavlovian Conditioning.

The following quotations (cf. p. 39) can perhaps help us to find out what we think about the problem of the scientist's ethical responsibility.

Answer the different questions and then let's find out together what we can say about the scientist's ethical responsibility!
(The quotations are taken from the book: "Science in the Modern World" – Hrsg. Mäcking/Penkwitt)

1) "...When he (Oppenheimer)...expresses his hope that we may reap the blessings of atomic energy rather than the whirlwind of misery, he spoke for the eternal scientist..." (p. 24)
   Question: Which quality does the author allude to, when he speaks of the "eternal scientist"?

2) "...scientific work must not be considered from the point of view of its direct usefulness. It must be done for itself, for the beauty of science, and then there is always the chance that a scientific discovery may become, like radium, a benefit for humanity." (p. 50)
   Question: Can you also imagine a different result if scientific work is done "for the beauty of science"?

3) "...If the past is any indication of the future, a nation, in order to lead in technology must lead in pure science. That in a few words is one compelling answer to the question, why more science?" (p. 66)
   Question: This statement is undoubtedly true. What about technological progress in "Brave New World"?

4) "...It appears that despite 'Brave New World Revisited' and all the other eloquent manifestations of his recognition of the dangers of a scientifically directed world, Huxley did, in fact, share the belief of our Scientific Age that rapid scientific progress is inevitable..."(p. 116)
   Question: Does a novel like "Brave New World" confirm the author's statement?

5) This quotation is taken from Huxley's "Brave New World Revisited" (p. 37): "The wish to impose order upon confusion, to bring harmony out of dissonance and unity out of multiplicity, is a kind of intellectual instinct, a primary and fundamental urge of the mind. Within the realms of science, art and philosophy, the workings of what I may call this *Will to Order,* are mainly beneficent."
   Question: Does Huxley justify unlimited research by saying that man's "intellectual instinct" and his "will to order" are "mainly beneficent"?

10. Stunde:
Sex and Soma in Brave New World

= Chpt. 15 (handschriftlich)

Zur didaktischen Funktion

Es soll im Verlauf dieser Stunde gezeigt werden, welche Funktion die Liberalisierung des Sexualverhaltens der Brave New Worlder hat. Der Slogan „Jeder gehört jedem" ist für das Funktionieren des Systems ebenso wichtig wie viele der sonstigen hypnopädischen Lehrsätze. Die Szene zwischen Lenina und John zeigt besonders eindringlich, daß das Fehlen jeglicher zwischenmenschlicher Beziehung sowie die strenge Trennung von Liebe und Sinnlichkeit den sexuellen Akt bedeutungslos machen und ihn auf dieselbe Ebene stellen wie das „Fühlkino" oder ähnliche oberflächlich-sinnliche Vergnügungen. Welchen erwünschten Nebeneffekt sexuelle Freizügigkeit im Sinne von BNW auch haben kann, darauf soll in der 13. Stunde noch eingegangen werden.

In der Stabilisierung des Gesamtsystems übernimmt die Glücksdroge Soma eine ganz ähnliche Funktion wie die reglementierte Promiskuität. Sie lenkt ab, läßt vergessen, wahrt die notwendige Oberflächlichkeit und ist somit ein weiterer, wichtiger Pfeiler im Gefüge der schönen, neuen Welt. Dennoch sollte Soma andrerseits auch als Schwachstelle des Systems erkannt werden. Funktionierte nämlich diese schöne, neue Welt wirklich so perfekt, wäre die Zufriedenheit wirklich so groß, müßte man eigentlich auf eine Droge des Vergessens verzichten können, sollte der Vergleich mit Alkohol- und Drogenmißbrauch in unserer Gesellschaft nicht möglich sein.

Die Szene, in der John versucht, die Deltas von der stumpfen Monotonie ihres Daseins zu befreien und ihnen die Motive ihres Handelns (bzw. ihrer „Sucht") klarzumachen, zeigt deutlich, daß John *Soma* zwar als Schwachstelle des Systems erkennt, daß es ihm aber unmöglich ist, die undurchdringliche Geschlossenheit des gesellschaftlichen Gefüges zu durchbrechen.

Ziele der Stunde

Die Schüler sollen

– erkennen, daß Sexualität und Promiskuität ohne zwischenmenschliche Beziehung bedeutungslos und systemfestigend geworden ist
– wissen, woher das Wort Soma kommt
– durch den Vergleich mit Alkohol- und Drogenmißbrauch in unserer Gesellschaft *Soma* als die Schwachstelle des Systems erkennen
– in der Lage sein, Johns Befreiungsversuch als Bestätigung dieser Vermutung und zugleich als sinnlose Revolte zu interpretieren

Verlaufsskizze

Voraussetzungen:

a) Die Schüler haben das Kapitel 13 (S. 190, "You don't seem very glad to see me…" bis S. 195, "…was accelerated like a pistolshot.") und das Kapitel 15 (S. 212, "But do you like being slaves?" bis S. 214, "…he tumbled on the floor.") gründlich gelesen.

b) Die Schüler haben sich zu Hause Notizen zu dem Thema: "Why do people become alcoholics or drug addicts?" gemacht.
   (Ein Schüler hat die Notizen auf Folie festgehalten.)

Unterrichtsschritt 1:

Im Unterrichtsgespräch soll zunächst versucht werden, den Zusammenhang zwischen vorgeschriebener Promiskuität und systemkonformem Denken herzustellen. Das Ergebnis wird an der Tafel festgehalten.

Unterrichtsschritt 2:

Als Überleitung zum Problemkomplex Soma folgt eine kurze Information des Lehrers über die Herkunft des Wortes.

Unterrichtsschritt 3:

Die Hausaufgabe hat ein Schüler auf Overhead-Folie festgehalten (Gründe für Alkoholismus und Drogenmißbrauch). Im gemeinsamen Gespräch werden Gründe für den Gebrauch von Soma dem gegenübergestellt, und die Schüler notieren sich das Ergebnis.

Unterrichtsschritt 4:

Als Auflockerung und besonders einprägsames Beispiel für eine spezielle Art des Drogenmißbrauchs kann hier der Song "Mother's Little Helper" von den Rolling Stones eingesetzt werden. (Text s. S. 42)

Unterrichtsschritt 5:

Während der Song abgespielt wird, schreibt der Lehrer die Leitfragen zu Kapitel 15 (S. 212–14) an die Tafel. Die Schüler beantworten diese Fragen in Stillarbeit; das Ergebnis wird besprochen und an der Tafel festgehalten.

Zum Inhalt der Stunde

Unterrichtsschritt 1:
The function of sex and sensuality

It is important to keep in mind that there is no meaningful human relationship among the Brave New Worlders, so sex and sensuality have become detached from their object. It is in this sense that we have to interpret the slogan "Everybody belongs to everybody else". In BNW sex and sensual pleasures are either of a narcisstic nature (feelies, scent organ etc.) or else, if directed towards another person, they always remain on a crudely sensual level, that will never be transcended into real love. Because of their conditioning and their sexual education (see also lesson 5 + 6), the Brave New Worlders are emotionally unable to transcend the stage of infantile eroticism, they remain "infants where feeling and desire are concerned" (p. 102). There's one scene that shows us particularly well what love has come to mean in BNW. In chapter 13 Lenina goes to see John, because she has fallen in love with him. John loves and admires her as well, but when the two are confronted once more, they cannot communicate. John wants pure and heroic love, he wants to show himself worthy of Lenina's love: "I wanted to do something first…" (p. 190). He fortifies himself against any kind of purely sexual desire by quoting Shakespeare: "…shall never melt mine honour into lust…", and as a ridiculously inadequate answer to John's noble passion, Lenina starts her confession of love: "I wanted you so much. And if you wanted me too, why didn't you…?" (p. 193) and she confirms her words by dropping her zippicamiknicks. The satirical description of the scene makes the tragic misunderstanding seem strangely comical and funny, but it certainly shows us one thing: sex in BNW has become absolutely meaningless, and must be seen on the same level as the feelies, the scent organ, or in fact any other kind of superficial distraction like Electromagnetic Golf.

Unterrichtsschritt 2:
Soma

Before we talk about *soma,* it's quite interesting to know why Huxley has chosen that name. *Soma* has two meanings: One is well-known, it's the Greek word for body. At the

41

same time *soma* is the name of a plant that has highly intoxicating effects and that, in old Indian rituals, was used as an offering to the Gods.

Unterrichtsschritt 3:
Soma, alcohol, and drugs

It's strange that there should be anything like *soma* in BNW, and when Mond says: "And if ever, by some unlucky chance, anything unpleasant should somehow happen, why, there's always *soma* to give you a holiday from the facts." (p. 235), he indirectly admits that the system is not quite as perfect as it ought to be. He's not right when he compares *soma* to "years of hard moral training" (p. 235), because he's unaware of the fact that moral training enables people to bear things, that it makes them independent, whereas *soma* can only give you a "holiday from the facts". The point of comparison would, rather, be alcohol or drugs. Like *soma,* alcohol and drugs are a flight from reality; people try to escape from the things they can't bear (escapism). However, there's one important difference: *Soma* is not detrimental to your health, it doesn't give you a hangover, and, because it has no negative after-effects, it won't cause social disaster. This is something, but we keep asking

Arbeitsblatt zur 10. Stunde

Mother's Little Helper

① 'Kids are different today,'
   I hear ev'ry mother say
   Mother needs something today to
      calm her down
   And though she's not really ill
   There's a little yellow pill
   She goes running for the shelter
      of a mother's little helper
   And it helps her on her way
   Gets her through her busy day.
   What a drag it is getting old.

② 'Kids are different today,'
   I hear ev'ry mother say
   Cooking fresh food, for a hus-
      band's just a drag
   So she buys an instant cake
   And she burns her frozen steak
   And goes running for the shelter
      of a mother's little helper
   And two help her on her way
   Get her through her busy day.
   What a drag it is getting old.

③ 'Kids aren't the same today,'
   I hear ev'ry mother say
   They just don't appreciate that you
      get tired
   They're so hard to satisfy
   You can tranquilise your mind
   So go running for the shelter of a
      mother's little helper
   And four help you through the night
   Help to minimise your plight.
   What a drag it is getting old.

④ 'Kids are much too hard today,'
   I hear ev'ry mother say
   The pursuit of happiness just
      seems a bore
   And if you take more of those
   You will get an overdose
   No more running to the shelter of
      a mother's little helper
   They just helped you on your way
   Through your busy dying day.
   What a drag it is getting old.

Words and Music by Mick Jagger and Keith Richard © Essex Musikvertrieb GmbH Köln

---

ourselves why people who have been perfectly conditioned to "love their unescapable social destiny" (p. 31) need *soma:* What do they have to escape from? In case there's a social misfit like Bernard who has got too much "alcohol in his blood-surrogate?" (p. 97); in case there's another odd person like John, who causes trouble? That can't be the only reason, when we consider a scene like John's revolt.

Unterrichtsschritt 4:
Mother's Little Helper

Cf. text on page 42

Unterrichtsschritt 5:
John's revolt

When, in all his grief, John leaves Park Lane Hospital, he suddenly finds himself in the midst of two Delta Bokanovsky Groups, the menial staff of the Hospital. They're about to get their daily *soma*-ration. The words of their song: "How many goodly creatures are there here. How beauteous mankind is! O brave new world…" (p. 209) makes John feel the derisive contrast between this miserable khaki mob and the original beauty of Miranda's words. "It was a challenge, a command." (p. 210). John wants to free these poor subhuman creatures, he wants them to revolt against the world that has made them slaves. A convincing scene, a further occasion where the reader is able to identify with John, where, like John, he forgets that the "bestial stupidity" (p. 212) of these subhuman beings, cannot, and will never be able, to grasp the meaning of great words like manhood and freedom. Their lives are not pleasant, they have not been sufficiently conditioned really to like their situation, but the daily ration of their "little helper" Soma, can make mankind seem 'beauteous', and the new world 'brave'. It's only when John and Helmholtz throw the soma ration out of the window that the Deltas show a human reaction: fury. Withdrawal symptoms? Anyway, the system doesn't work any more, and a complete breakdown can only be avoided by 'somatizing' the whole battle-field. So, after all, Soma is more than an expedient, it's an important part of the system, showing the practical deficiencies of an apparently perfect theory.

Sequenz 4: Human Nature in Conflict with the Brave New World

11./12. Stunde:
A "Perfect" System

Zur didaktischen Funktion

Nachdem bisher in den vorausgegangenen Stunden das in BNW herrschende Gesellschaftssystem ausführlich besprochen wurde, werden nun anhand des 16. Kapitels die Schwachstellen des Systems thematisiert.

Als Einstieg in die Stunde dient die Frage nach den Tricks, die der Autor anwenden muß, um Bewegung in eine Welt zu bringen, die völlig statisch angelegt ist.

Als Ergebnis sollte festgehalten werden, daß von zwei Seiten dem System Gefahren drohen können: Konfliktquellen im System selbst (in diesem Fall die α-Intellektuellen) und Bedrohungen von außen (in der Person Johns). In dieser Doppelstunde werden nun zunächst die „systemimmanenten" Gefahren, die α-Intellektuellen, besprochen, während die Bedrohung von außen (Konfliktträger ist John) in der nächsten Stunde abgehandelt wird.

Aufgefächert wird zunächst noch einmal das perfekte Kastenwesen, auf dem die soziale Stabilität der Brave New World sich gründet (dazu dient ein Ausschnitt aus dem zentralen Disput zwischen M. Mond, Helmholtz Watson und John im 16. Kapitel), daran anschließend wird die Rolle der α-Intellektuellen problematisiert. Es wird herausgearbeitet, daß hier eine potentielle Konfliktquelle ist, aber im Gegenzug klargemacht, wie das System die Gefahr, die von diesen Intellektuellen ausgeht, zu neutralisieren versteht. Eine Charakterisierung Bernard Marx' und Helmholtz Watsons macht zusätzlich deutlich, wie gering die Gefahr ist, die von diesen Individuen ausgeht.

Ziele der Stunde

Die Schüler sollen
- erkennen, welche Ereignisse und Personen Bewegung in das perfekte System von BNW bringen
- M. Monds Argumente für die Notwendigkeit des Kastensystems in BNW kennen und kritisch bewerten können
- wissen, auf welche besondere Weise α-Individuen konditioniert werden müssen.
- Bernhard Marx und Helmholtz Watson charakterisieren können und erkennen, daß ihre Außenseiterposition verschiedene Ursachen hat.

Verlaufsskizze

Voraussetzungen:

Der Text auf S. 219–22 ist gründlich gelesen, und die Leitfragen (siehe Stundenblatt) wurden beantwortet.

Unterrichtsschritt 1:

Die Frage nach den dramaturgischen Problemen des Autors wird vom Lehrer zunächst näher erläutert und dann von den Schülern in Stillarbeit beantwortet. Die Ergebnisse werden besprochen und an der Tafel festgehalten. (Siehe T. A.)

Unterrichtsschritt 2:

Die Hausaufgabe (S. 219–22, Die Frage nach dem Kastensystem) wird in Form eines Unterrichtsgesprächs abgerufen; und die Ergebnisse werden an der Tafel festgehalten.

Unterrichtsschritt 3:

Der Text auf S. 101–103 (von "Everyone says I'm awfully pneumatic..." bis "...I wish he weren't so odd.") wird mit verteilten Rollen gelesen, daran schließt sich ein kurzes Unterrichtsgespräch zur Charakterisierung der α-Intellektuellen an.

Unterrichtsschritt 4:

Mit Hilfe des Textes auf S. 79–81 und aufgrund der Kenntnis des gesamten Romans charakterisieren zwei Gruppen von Schülern je eines der beiden Individuen Bernard Marx und Helmholtz Watson. Die Ergebnisse der Gruppenarbeit werden an der Tafel festgehalten.

Zusätzliche Diskussionspunkte

– Könnte man sich alternative „Störfaktoren" für den Roman vorstellen?
– Welche Charaktereigenschaften können zu abweichendem Verhalten führen?
– Sind Watson und Marx überzeugende Charaktere?

Zum Inhalt der Stunde

Unterrichtsschritt 1:
The author's techniques of introducing conflict

BNW's perfectly standardized and stable society could be compared to an impenetrable circle. The members of this perfect system are within the circle and are normally not given the chance to peer above the walls of their world. If the author wants to show us that, despite all its perfection, the new world is inhuman and despicable, he must try to penetrate the circle either by introducing some distracting elements from the outside, or by deliberately constructing a mistake inside the system. What are the devices Huxley uses to make latent conflicts become apparent? The first condition is that, apart from BNW, there must exist a different world to which it can be compared. The author must then connect the two worlds either by sending somebody out to see the other world, or by introducing someone from this other world. And, as a third condition, there must be some misfits in BNW who are sufficiently "de-conditioned" to be interested in finding fault with the system.

As an alternative to BNW Huxley created the Reservation. The link between BNW and the Reservation is the DHC's and Linda's excursion to that place and the "accident" they had there. John, the Director's and Linda's son must, by his very birth, be considered a "hybrid" between a Brave New Worlder and a Savage. The fundamental conflict is established by getting the two outsiders – Bernard Marx and Helmholtz Watson – into contact with John.

Unterrichtsschritt 2:
Mond's justification of the caste-system

It has always been a dream of racists and some dangerously naïve perfectionists to create a perfect race, a race of "Alpha Double Pluses" (p. 220). But it is rather horror and pity with the Bokanovsky twins that induce John to suggest a world where everybody would be an Alpha Double Plus. Mond, however, is far beyond John's naïve proposal, he knows very well, that a "society of Alphas couldn't fail to be unstable and miserable" (p. 220). The "Cyprus Experiment" (p. 221/22) proved long ago that a society can only function *and be stable* if everyone is assigned the place he's fit for: A place for everyone and everyone in his place. A familiar argument that has often been used to justify class distinction in our society as well. There's one great difference, however, between a conservative justification of class distinction in our world, and Mond's explanation of BNW's caste-system: when he compars the socialization and conditioning of Alphas and Epsilons to bottles, his picture definitely excludes any kind of social mobility. Whether the bottles are small or enormous, miserable or comfortable, they have one thing in common: they cannot be broken. Their "inhabitants" will neither be allowed social ascendence nor will they be threatened with social descent. They can move inside the bottle, according to the space they're given, but even the walls of their bottles are blurred by their conditioning ("I dont want to play with Delta children. And Epsilons are still worse... I'm so glad I'm a Beta...", p. 42) that makes them unable and unwilling to look into the bottles of their lower or higher caste fellow-men.

Unterrichtsschritt 3:
Neutralizing α-individuals

Lenina's and Bernard's flight to Amsterdam is their first outing together, and not a very jolly one either. Bernard, the intelligent misfit, who doesn't "respond properly to conditioning" (p. 97), but whose job it is to condition other people (he works in the hypnopaedic department), seems rather gloomy and sulky, when compared to Lenina. Lenina is a beautiful example of a synthetic mass-produced human being: perfect body, perfect conditioning, perfectly trained behaviour. In her eyes, Bernard must be "pretty disquieting" (p. 97): "...that mania for doing things in private", his complete lack of sociability, his refusal to take *soma,* his cynical comment on Lenina's treasure of sleep-taught wisdom and, worst of all, his love of

wild and untouched nature ("walk for a couple of hours in the heather" p. 97, "look at the sea in peace, p. 99). Lenina can't possibly answer Bernard's blasphemous remarks and questions, and Bernard should know that better than anyone else. His attempts to break through Lenina's thought conditioning only corroborates her determination to "preserve her incomprehension intact". (p. 100). Alphas and Betas must necessarily be kept at the stage of infants "where feeling and desire are concerned" (p. 102); infants whose innocence consists in their firm belief in hypnopaedic platitudes, their immediate satisfaction of purely physical needs, and their unquestioning acceptance of BNW's rules.

Unterrichtsschritt 4:
Characterization of Watson and Marx

Marx:
In the helicopter scene we got to know Bernard as a gloomy person who is ill at ease in the perfect new world. Compared to Lenina, with her over-adjustment and the bright treasure of her sleep-taught wisdom however, he seems fallible but at least human. What's the root of Bernard's discontent? We know that his physique is "hardly better than the average Gamma" (p. 75) and that his physical inadequacy makes him rather self-conscious and introverted. He's painfully aware of his atypical appearance and he can't accept it. It's some kind of unfortunate accident that made him different from his fellow-men. The development of character will show that his critical attitude towards BNW is nothing but the result of this physical shortcoming. He has always been longing to be one of *them,* and as soon as he is given the chance to have any girl he wants, as soon as he can mistake people's interest in John for an interest in his own person, "success goes fizzily to Bernard's head" (p. 159), he suddenly likes the world that he had criticized and hated, he drops Helmholtz-Watson, he thoroughly en-

joys his "sense of importance" (p. 159), and he completely forgets what he had suffered from all his life: the consciousness of being seperate. He's nothing but an ill-humoured conformist, he has lost any claim to be a hero or a revolutionist, and the reader is well-prepared for the miserable, cowardly and green-faced Bernard he will encounter in Mond's office.

Helmholtz Watson:
Just like Bernard, Helmholtz Watson doesn't feel quite at ease in BNW. The roots of his discontent, however, are of a quite different nature. He's a "powerfully built man... handsome and... every centimetre an Alpha-Plus" (p. 77). He's successful and women like him, but another imperfection in the system has made him "a little too able" (p. 78). Using Mustapha Mond's picture, we could say that his bottle is too small for him. He feels the power to write things that BNW has no use for. He's frustrated, because he has got the intellectual powers of an artist whose raw-material, like love, passion, heroism, suffering and real happiness, has been taken away. More than his upbringing should allow for, he understands the Savage, he appreciates Shakespeare, and he's convinced that John's attempt to free the Deltas from their unworthy existence is justified. He's one of a number of Alpha-Pluses who is sufficiently strong and intelligent to overcome his conditioning, to "break their bottle", and to menace the system. Mond knows very well, that, with a man like that he has only got the choice either to send him to an island, or take him on to the staff of "the Controllers", with the prospect of succeeding in due course to an actual Controllership (p. 225).

13. Stunde:
Dangers to the Stability of the System

Zur didaktischen Funktion

Diese Stunde schließt sich inhaltlich eng an die vorangegangene an, da nun der bis jetzt ausgesparte Teil des zentralen Disputs zwischen M. Mond, Helmholtz Watson und John besprochen wird, in dem als weiterer Konfliktträger John in der Auseinandersetzung mit dem wichtigsten Repräsentanten von BNW, Mond, vorgestellt wird. Der unmittelbare Anlaß für diesen Teil der Diskussion ist ein Shakespeare-Zitat, das John dazu bringt, seine Kritik an BNW offen zu äußern. Der Name Shakespeare steht stellvertretend für Kunst überhaupt, und der Inhalt des Gesprächs besteht im wesentlichen in M. Monds These, daß Kreativität – ebenso wie Geschichte, Wissenschaft und Ethik – mit sozialer Stabilität unvereinbar sind.
Zwei Dinge sollten geklärt werden, damit die Schüler dem Gang des Gesprächs folgen können:
Zunächst muß ein so abstrakter Begriff wie "high art" etwas konkretisiert werden. Hierfür bietet sich an, die Schüler anhand von Namen und Titeln, die ihnen bekannt sind, Kriterien für die Verwendung des Begriffs finden zu lassen.
Außerdem sollte man an dieser Stelle kurz auf die Bedeutung der Freudschen Sublimationstheorie eingehen und versuchen, den Zusammenhang zwischen der unmittelbaren Befriedigung sexueller Bedürfnisse und dem Fehlen jeglicher Kreativität herzustellen.
John kann Monds Erklärung dafür, daß Kunst in BNW keinen Platz hat, natürlich nicht überzeugen, weil er bereits die Prämisse "Happiness is the sovereign good" nicht akzeptiert. Er macht seinen Anspruch auf Unglück, Tragik und Mühsal geltend. Die

schöne neue Welt ist ihm zu oberflächlich, und sein Scheitern auf der Suche nach einem Ausweg muß auf dem Hintergrund dieses Gesprächs gesehen werden.

Ziele der Stunde

Die Schüler sollen
- versuchen, Kriterien für die Verwendung des Begriffs "high art" zu finden, und sollen erkennen, weshalb der Begriff in BNW keinen Platz haben kann
- wissen, was man unter dem Freudschen Begriff Sublimation versteht und auf welche Weise auch dieser Teil von Freuds Theorie in das System von BNW integriert wurde
- erkennen, warum Johns Selbstmord unvermeidbar ist

Verlaufsskizze

Voraussetzungen:

Alle Schüler haben Kapitel 16, S. 218/19 von "Why don't you let them see…" bis "…a lot of agreeable sensations to the audience" und Kapitel 17, S. 235–37 von "but tears are necessary…" bis "you're welcome, he said." gründlich gelesen.

Unterrichtsschritt 1:

Mit Hilfe von Dias, einer Hektographie oder einer Folie für den Overhead-Projektor werden den Schülern verschiedene Buchtitel, Theaterstücke, Bilder etc. vorgeführt, die ihnen bekannt sind, und von denen sie zunächst nur bestimmen sollen, ob es sich dabei um "high art" handelt oder nicht.

Unterrichtsschritt 2:

In Stillarbeit überlegen und notieren sich die Schüler die Kriterien, die sie bei ihrer Kategorisierung stillschweigend zugrunde gelegt haben. Besprechung der Stillarbeit; Festhalten der Ergebnisse an der Tafel.

Unterrichtsschritt 3:

In einem kurzen Lehrervortrag werden die Schüler über Freuds Begriff der Sublimation informiert.

Unterrichtsschritt 4:

Im schülerzentrierten Unterrichtsgespräch soll Johns Position (S. 235–37) und sein zwangsläufiger Weg in den Selbstmord noch einmal zusammengefaßt und analysiert werden.

Zusätzliche Diskussionspunkte

- Wäre Selbstmord für einen Brave New Worlder denkbar?
- Vergleich von feelies etc. mit Trivialliteratur und seichten Unterhaltungsfilmen

Zum Inhalt der Stunde

Zu Unterrichtsschritt 1 + 2:
"High Art"

In John's opinion Shakespeare's plays are not only one of the finest examples of Western literature; they are everything the term "high art" can possibly stand for. Opposed to the artificial sterility of Brave New World, the perfection of the work of art, the shape of the artist's phantasy show us what passion, suffering, heroism and nobility can be. "High art" is the expression of everything Helmholtz Watson is unable to find in his world. Even if there are no absolute criteria to measure the beauty of the work of art, its creation requires certain conditions that BNW cannot supply: sincerity and genuine feelings. It's the sincere and poetic expression of what life really is that John is missing in the feelies and the scent organ. John's judgement about them – "they don't mean anything" (p. 219) – expresses BNW's emotional emptiness, where there's no room for anything like "high art". In a strictly utilitarian society, everything must be part of the great machine and must fit into the system. "They mean themselves" (p. 219), is Mond's answer, and he wants to say that they are just another (necessary) distraction that could be replaced by any other superficial pleasure.

John's acquaintance with Shakespeare's plays... provides an external measure by which to evaluate the quality of existence in utopia, and if the reader uses this yardstick, he'll realize with a slight shudder that the very claim to perfection must turn any utopia into a horrible nightmare.

Zu Unterrichtsschritt 3:
Sublimation

"Sublimation was Freud's hope for the creative future of humanity" (Stafford-Clarke, p. 164). Art as the result of man's repressed sexual desire, this is what the term 'sublimation' has often been boiled down to. It's not as simple as all that, but in his "Introductory Lectures on Psychoanalysis", Freud does trace a path "from phantasy to reality – the path of art" (p. 165). Freud's concept of libido, however, implies more than just sexual desire, and he also admits different sources that contribute to the creation of the work of art. Taking these things into account, we can say that Freud believed the creation of the work of art to be – at least partly – due to the fact that the artist tries to transfer his dissatisfaction with reality, his repressed desires, in short, his libidinal energy to the construction of his life of phantasy, which he is then able to

transform into the work of art. So, according to Freud, artistic creation is the best way to cope with (i.e. to sublimate) an imperfect reality, inaccessible desires and impending neurosis. BNW's clever ideologists, however, succeeded in abolishing the very conditions for any kind of artistic creation. They picked out some of Freud's ideas and applied them at random, to form the basis of their sexual education: no families, infantile eroticism, complete and decreed promiscuity, plenty of sensual pleasures – anything to avoid the painful gap between reality and phantasy, anything to avoid the BNWorlders attempt to bridge that gap by creating some work of art.

Zu Unterrichtsschritt 4:
John's claim to be unhappy and
his final failure

At the beginning of the central dispute, we noticed that John was just putting questions that allowed Mond to expound his (i.e. BNW's) ideology. Mond rebuffed any kind of counter-argument by referring to BNW's "closed society". It's only towards the end of chapter 17 that John frankly makes a stand against Mond's world and defends his own notions. By claiming "the right to be unhappy" (p. 237) he attacks the essence of BNW's ideology, because happiness is social stability, happiness is the "Sovereign Good" (p. 178), happiness is what the world controller must constantly "think about" (p. 179) and it's for the sake of happiness and well-being that the whole complicated machinery is set in motion.

When we come to think of it, we can't help agreeing with John's criticism: "everything is too easy... nothing costs enough" (p. 236). But have John's words really convinced us? Is he convinced himself? The "long silence" (p. 237) that follows Mond's answer leaves us in doubt about it. It's rather easy to claim an abstract, poetical kind of unhappiness, but as soon as you have to choose between terrible

49

diseases ("cancer, typhoid, syphilis", p. 237), a hard struggle for life, the decay of the human body, and happiness – however limited and superficial it may be – the choice becomes difficult, if not tragic. This is perhaps the only occasion where even the reader must appreciate that Mond might have good reasons for establishing "happiness as the Sovereign Good", even at a "fairly high price" (p. 228). Furthermore, Mond's answer could hint at John's failure. Mond knows very well that John has no alternative. Going back to the Reservation would not only mean disease and more than primitive surroundings, it would also mean that he would have to live the life of an outcast, that he would be hated and persecuted.

Neither is he allowed to join Marx or Helmholtz Watson in their exile, for the simple reason that a dissident's life on an island is not supposed to be alternative. They are deliberately isolated, and the lack of community and solidarity will soon drown their aspirations for a better life.

John's own plan, the life of a hermit "just round the corner of civilization", is also doomed to failure. The BNWorlders' sensationalism, their incapacity to understand, much less tolerate a form of life that is opposed to all their conditioning and their beliefs will never give John the chance to find his peace of mind and to escape the putrefying contamination of a decadent civilization.

John commits suicide because his situation is desperate, because he's driven to choose between insanity (= the Reservation) on the one hand and lunacy (= BNW) on the other. Insofar as he escapes the world he loathes, his suicide must be called a failure, but insofar as it confirms his active (rejection) of this world, it could also be called a last act of bravado that shows the intensity of his hatred.

Contrary to what Huxley himself says in his foreword, he could *not* have offered John a "third alternative" (p. 9), because the very structure of this kind of utopian society doesn't allow for a third alternative. For all its "happiness" BNW is a totalitarian world state, and its leaders can't afford to show their subjects (and the reader) that it is not necessarily the best of all possible worlds.

14./15. Stunde:
Human Nature in Conflict with the Brave New World

Zur didaktischen Funktion

In der abschließenden Doppelstunde soll der Roman als Ganzes noch einmal besprochen werden.

Diese Zusammenfassung setzt zwei Schwerpunkte:

a) Die literarische Form der Satire und ihre spezielle Ausprägung in Huxleys Roman

b) Huxleys später hinzugefügtes Vorwort, als Kritik und Rechtfertigung seines Romans

Schon bei der Charakterisierung der Personen werden die Schüler sehr schnell merken, wie flach und beinahe marionettenhaft die verschiedenen Charaktere sind. Damit liegt bereits *ein* wichtiges Merkmal der Satire fest:

– Die Charaktere sind überzeichnet und wirken dadurch wenig lebensecht. Im Zusammenhang mit den Charakteren muß natürlich auch deren Namensgebung als wichtiges satirisches Element miteinbezogen werden.

– Ein weiteres Kennzeichen der Satire ist der ironisch-distanzierte Stil des Autors, auf den bei der Besprechung des ersten Kapitels bereits kurz hingewiesen wurde und der anhand eines Textabschnittes in dieser Stunde genauer untersucht werden soll.

– Schließlich sollte man zum Abschluß auch

noch einmal auf das eingehen, was in der ersten Stunde über den Titel des Buches gesagt wurde.

Die Zusammenstellung all dieser Merkmale soll es den Schülern ermöglichen, BNW als Zwitterform zwischen Satire und Thesenroman zu erkennen. Huxleys *Vorwort,* das 14 Jahre nach der Erstveröffentlichung des Romans geschrieben wurde, könnte man als nachträgliche, den Zeitumständen angepaßte Kritik des Autors an seinem eigenen Werk verstehen. Gezielte Fragen versetzen die Schüler in die Lage, das inhaltliche Gerüst des Vorwortes wie folgt festzuhalten:

1. Huxley kritisiert die Tatsache, daß er John keine wirkliche Alternative ermöglicht hat.
2. Der Autor begründet, weshalb er die Atombombe (das physikalische Phänomen der Atomspaltung war im Jahre 1932 bereits bekannt) nicht in das Geschehen des Romans miteinbezogen hat.
3. Vom Dreißigjährigen Krieg über den ersten Weltkrieg bis hin zum Faschismus des Dritten Reichs läßt Huxley die europäische Geschichte Revue passieren und kommt, trotz der vagen Hoffnung, daß die Menschheit etwas aus ihrem Schicksal gelernt habe, schließlich zu der
4. zwangsläufigen Entstehung eines totalitären Weltstaats. Die umwälzenden Veränderungen, die vor allem die Atomphysik mit sich bringen wird, können, so Huxley, nur von einem stark zentralisierten, totalitären Regime getragen werden. Einer Regierung, die sich durch die im Roman dargestellten Mittel (genetische Manipulation, Konditionierung etc.) ein Volk von zufriedenen Sklaven geschaffen hat.

Noch steht der Menschheit die Möglichkeit offen, die „Wohlstandstyrannei" der schönen neuen Welt abzuwenden. Aber beide Faktoren, die Atombombe und die Möglichkeiten genetischer Manipulation, sind heute weitaus gefährlicher geworden, als das im Jahr 1946 der Fall war. Der Zeitpunkt, an dem wir nur noch zwischen „1984" oder „Brave New World" wählen können, scheint noch näher gerückt: "You pays your money and you takes your choice" (Huxley-Foreword)

Ziele der Stunde

Die Schüler sollen

– erkennen, warum die Charaktere in „BNW" etwas hölzern und eindimensional wirken und warum sich der Leser nur schwer mit ihnen identifizieren kann
– wissen, woher die Namen der Personen abgeleitet sind und was diese Namengebung bedeutet
– Huxleys Stil als ein wichtiges Element der Satire analysieren können
– in der Lage sein, Merkmale der Satire zu nennen und „BNW" in dieses Raster einzuordnen
– Huxleys Vorwort als Kritik und Rechtfertigung des Autors verstehen und zusammenfassen können

Verlaufsskizze

Voraussetzungen:

Die Schüler haben die Charakterisierung der wichtigsten Personen im Roman vorbereitet und ein Arbeitsblatt mit Inhaltsfragen zum Vorwort (s. S. 56) beantwortet. (Diese Fragen sollten gruppenweise verteilt werden.)

Unterrichtsschritt 1:

Zunächst werden einige der zu Hause vorbereiteten Charakterisierungen (ohne Kommentar des Lehrers) vorgelesen.

Unterrichtsschritt 2:

Im Unterrichtsgespräch wird festgestellt, weshalb die Charaktere so flach sind und was die (ironische) Namensgebung des Autors bedeutet.

Unterrichtsschritt 3 + 4:

Nachdem im Unterrichtsgespräch einige Stichworte zu den Begriffen Satire, Ironie etc. gegeben wurden, lesen die Schüler in Stillarbeit den Textabschnitt auf S. 29/30 und versuchen, Huxleys Stil zu beschreiben und mit Beispielen zu belegen. Das Ergebnis der Stillarbeit wird besprochen und an der Tafel festgehalten. (Siehe T.A.)

Unterrichtsschritt 5:

Besprechung der Hausaufgabe (Fragen auf dem Arbeitsblatt), die Beiträge werden an der Tafel gesammelt. (Siehe T.A.)

Erweiterungsmöglichkeiten

– Äußerungen verschiedener Autoren zu "BNW" werden den Schülern vorgelegt und diskutiert.
– Ist Huxleys Begründung dafür, daß er die Atombombe außer acht gelassen hat, überzeugend?
– Vergleich von "BNW" mit anderen Utopien (vor allem Orwells „1984").

Zum Inhalt der Stunde

Zu Unterrichtsschritt 1 + 2:
The characters and their names

Lenina:
is a well-conditioned, pretty and fairly successful product of BNW. Her idea of sex has been reduced to something between neutral pleasure and infantile narcissism. John's at-tempt to cast such a 'product' into the role of Miranda or Juliet must therefore seem all the more inadequate and ridiculous. Lenina's character is rather a good example of the conditions that BNW conditioning requires. As soon as she has to face any difficulties (the Reservation, John etc.), her conditioning starts to crack and she resorts to *soma.*

Lenina's marxist name (see also Bernard Marx, Polly Trotsky etc.) is satirical in two respects: just like all the other Brave New Worlders, Lenina can't have any idea of Russian history ("History is bunk"); the reader's knowledge of history, however, will make the contrast even more ludicrous: Lenin, the Party intellectual, and Lenina, the naive and well-adjusted puppet of an artificial world.

Bernard Marx:
In the eleventh and twelfth lesson, Bernard has already been characterized and contrasted with Helmholtz Watson. His vain longing for conformism and success and the dissatisfaction that he tries to transform into rebellion against the system satirically justifiy his name: Karl Marx the intellectual who attacked capitalism with his powerful thoughts, and Bernard Marx, the intelligent weakling whose lack of success and envy of the well-adjusted induce him to attack BNW's Fordist society and account for the very failure of his attempt.

Helmholtz Watson:
Watson's name is a curious amalgamation of the name of a German scientist: Hermann Ludwig von Helmholtz (1821–1935) and an English poet: Sir William Watson (1858–1935). Only slightly satirical this time, because, as an emotional engineer of the feelies and other distractions, Watson does indeed have the function of someone who is between a scientist and a poet. But what have science and poetry come to be? Cheap stuff, words and feelings about "nothing... that's what it finally boils down to..." (p. 81).

Watson himself knows that his creative urge is incompatible with BNW's emotional emptiness, and even with John's help, he'll never be able to write about things that matter, or to write for people who could understand him.

The Savage:
Does he play the role of Rousseau's "bon sauvage" – a sound contrast to a decaying civilization? Or is he the only one who, despite his name, has had the chance to remain "civilized", while the rest of humanity has been turned into functional robots? Can the reader identify with John? We can't find a definite answer to any of these questions, because John is a little bit of everything, but he's not very convincing in any of these roles. First of all, John is not really part of the Reservation; as the son of Brave New Worlders, he has never been completely integrated into the world of mystery, rituals and passion. His acquaintance with Shakespeare's plays helps the reader to compare BNW's cold technology to Shakespeare's deeply human passions, but John's interpretation and understanding of Shakespeare seem highly improbable for someone who discovered the books by mere chance and could hardly have possessed an adequate knowledge of the language to read, much less understand them. Had he really understood what these plays were about, he would certainly not have taken so long to realize that Lenina can neither be Miranda nor Juliet, that the Deltas will never revolt against the system, and that even Helmholtz is simply unable to understand the old world's conflicts.

Just like the reader, John is introduced into an unknown world, but he's slow to see what happens, and when he does, it's too late. It is his very naivety and his ingenuous attitude that keep the reader from identifying with him.

Mustapha Mond:
If he has been conceived as John's counterpart, Huxley could certainly be accused of favouring BNW's system. Mustapha Mond is clever, wordly-wise, subtle and cynical. He knows exactly what he's about, what he and his people have to dispense with, if they want to preserve "happiness", their "sovereign good". In his discussion with John, he would certainly have been able to transcend the limits of BNW, but he's clever enough to see that John's naivety is not really worth going to such intellectual lengths over, and that he can easily take the wind out of John's sails by telling him that times have changed, that his ideas are antiquated and obsolete, and that no Brave New Worlder will ever understand or appreciate his values.

In a satirical novel like "BNW", the characters cannot be different from what they are. Genuine Brave New Worlders are like puppets or robots, and must be considered the main objects of satire. Even misfits, dissidents and outsiders are too weak, too 'blurred', and too restricted in their impact to be convincing.

Unterrichtsschritt 3 a:
BNW, a satire?

"BNW depends, like all satire, upon the existence of commonly held values and attitudes which it presents as violated or perverted by the thing satirized." (Insight II, p. 1178)
Commonly held values are: the respect of life and death, the love of one's fellow men, the "pursuit of happiness", the invulnerability and uniqueness of the individual, the freedom to choose one's religion and hold one's own beliefs, and, of course, the tacit assumption that language is still a reliable instrument to communicate and to guarantee the maintenance of these values. In "BNW Revisited", Huxley mentions the manipulation of language as one of the most important characteristics of any totalitarian system: "In their anti-rational propaganda the enemies of freedom systematically pervert the resources of language in order to wheedle or stampede

their victims into thinking, feeling and acting as they, the mind-manipulators, want them to think, feel and act." ("BNW Revisited", p. 146/147)

In BNW, as well, language has lost its significance, the words have been emptied and distorted to the point of meaning the exact opposite of what they should stand for (e.g.: identity, history, happiness etc.). This distortion of language can be detected throughout the novel and is one of the most important elements of any satire: the author ridicules his targets by means of irony, i.e. by saying the opposite of what he thinks. The best example of the satirical use of language is the book's title, the word 'brave' implying any meaning from horrible and ghastly to – maybe – inevitable. Could Huxley ever have shown the reader his disgust at an over-technicized, superficial and emotionally impoverished world, had he not chosen satire as the most subtle and aggressive way of expressing it?

A closer look at any one of the pages will point out to us that his ironical style is an indispensable means of conveying BNW's atmosphere and the author's implied criticism of it at one and the same time.

Unterrichtsschritt 3 b:
Huxley's satirical style

As an example, let's have a look at page 29–31:

words like: blood-surrogate, revolution counter, oxygen shortage, heredity etc. suggest serious scientific methods that have been used for the benefit of mankind. "Nothing like oxygen shortage for keeping..." (p. 29). It's at this point that we expect to hear what this technological progress has been used for, and, just like the "ingenuous student" (p. 29), we're wondering why "keeping an embryo below par" (p. 29) is considered a scientific achievement. As we're not yet familiar with BNW's system and its logic, Huxley's ironical

remark "it evidently hadn't occurred to him" (p. 29) applies to the reader as well, as it hasn't occurred to him, either.

Hardly recovered from this shock, he (the reader) has to face Foster's disdainful way of talking about human beings as if they were trashy objects "... who are no use at all" (p. 29). Foster's enthusiasm and eagerness are sincere, just like the student's craving for knowledge, but subtly mocked at by Huxley's scornful aloofness: "Consider the horse. They considered it." (p. 30) Just in case the reader should still be in doubt about the author's position, he can find more of Huxley's ironical and hence false approval of Foster's convictions: "'...in Epsilons', said Mr Foster *very justly,* 'we don't need human intelligence'... Foster's enthusiasm was *infectious.*" (p. 30) Huxley seems to comment on that fact by using a word like "infectious" in the sense of "catching", but with all the negative connotations like disease, dirt, nausea etc.

Throughout the novel, the author maintains his position of a cool, ironical observer who describes a monstrous world of ridiculous puppets that have come to mistake their lunacy for the normal state of things. There's just one person who occasionally shares the role of the author, and that is Mond himself, for instance when he confuses the D.H.C. by saying: "It's all right, Director... I won't corrupt them" (p. 49), or when he encourages John to talk by surprising him with his good-humoured irony: "So you don't much like civilization, Mr. Savage..." (p. 217).

The most striking examples of Huxley's detached, satirical style can be found in the scenes where he shows an orthodox Brave New Worlder's behaviour as being absolutely inconsistent with some of the dissidents' ideas, as for instance in chapter 13, when Lenina comes to see John, and when they're talking at cross-purposes about their respective ideas of love, or when John goes to Park Lane Hospital and gives a rebuff to the nurse who's trying to make friendly small-talk (chapter 14) and, last but not least, the final discussion, where John's ideals and claims come up against Mond's superior contempt and BNW's hard facts: "…Nothing costs enough here (Twelve and a half million dollars, Henry Forster had protested when the Savage told him that. Twelve and a half million, that's what the new Conditioning Centre cost. Not a cent less.)"

Unterrichtsschritt 4:
Huxley's foreword

Huxley's foreword can be considered as the author's criticism and justification of his own novel, 14 years after the book's first publication. It may roughly be subdivided into four different sections:

1) According to the author, the most serious defect of the story is that the Savage is not given chance to escape from BNW's factitious civilization. When the novel was written in 1932, the author's satirical cynicism did not allow for the reasonable and human solution he now suggests in his foreword, and which sounds like a mixture between the prospects in his later utopian novel "Island" and Skinner's "Walden Two". (See also lesson 3 + 4)

2) The phenomenon of nuclear fission and the possible consequences of atomic energy were already well-known by the year 1932. Huxley frankly qualifies the fact that nuclear energy is not even mentioned as an "obvious failure of foresight" (p. 10). In contrast to what he thinks about the first "defect of the story" (p. 7), – i.e. the Savage's deadlock –, however, he's quick to explain his "oversight" (p. 10): just like many other branches of science, atomic physics only affects the outer conditions of human life, not its inner quality. "BNW" however is concerned with the "final and most searching revolution" (p. 11) which is neither political nor economic, nor even psychological in the tra-

ditional sense. It's concerned with the "truly revolutionary revolution" (p. 11), i.e. the complete manipulation of the individual by means of "genetic engineering" and pre-natal conditioning. The prospect of atomic warfare, however, would dispense with any kind of science fiction, we would not "have to bother with prophecies about the future" (p. 12).

3) Reviewing European history from the Thirty Years War to the horrors of the Second World War, Huxley comes to the conclusion that the horrors of ruinous warfare might deter mankind from causing another universal disaster, and that we might hope for a period "not indeed of peace, but of limited and only partially ruinous warfare" (p. 12). The chief stress would then necessarily be laid on technological progress and the industrial use of nuclear energy. This would entail a radical change of society: "far from painless operations that will be directed by highly centralized totalitarian governments" (p. 13).

4) It is this conviction that leads us to the fourth and last point of Huxley's foreword, where he comes back to his actual subject: a totalitarian state, able to deal with the "economic and social confusion" (p. 13) that will be the inevitable result of technological advance. The kind of government and society he then describes is the one we've just read about: an "all-powerful executive of political bosses" (p. 13/14), i.e. the World Controllers, who control a population of – voluntary – "slaves" (p. 14). The newly established centralized government uses four devices to make the slaves "love their servitude" (p. 14):

1) Thorough conditioning (Behaviourism)
2) A rigid caste-system
3) A drug for oblivion and pleasure *(soma)*

4) The standardization of human beings by means of eugenic manipulation.

Thirty-four years after the publication of Huxley's foreword, his prophecy that "the horror may be upon us within a single century" (p. 16) seems a bit out of date. "All things" – particularly recent experiments in genetics – "considered" (p. 16), it might not be another five years until we'll all have to face the consequences of "applied science... as the end to which human beings are to be made the means" (p. 16). Huxley's admonition to decentralize governmental power and to watch the application of scientific progress closely should at least make us sceptical about the future development of our modern world. Have we still got the chance to prevent the "welfare tyranny of Utopia"? (p. 16).

Arbeitsblatt zur 14./15. Stunde

---

1) p. 7/8
What, according to Huxley, is the most serious defect of his novel, and why?

2) p. 8
In which respect is the Savage not convincing?

3) p. 9/10
a) What would be the "third possibility" Huxley would offer the Savage?
b) What would this world be like?

4) p. 10/11
a) What – according to Huxley – was an "obvious failure of foresight?" What is missing in the novel?
b) How does he explain this deficiency? (p. 9/10)

5) p. 11
How can the "really revolutionary revolution" only be brought about?

6) p. 11
What does Huxley say about de Sade, and why can his Brave New Worlders not be compared to him?

7) p. 12/13
What does Huxley see as a possible consequence of the Second World War?

8) p. 12/13
Why will future governments (inevitably) have to be totalitarian?

9) p. 13/14
How can the efficiency of the modern totalitarian state be guaranteed?

10) p. 13–15
What are the methods Huxley suggests to make modern citizens fit in properly?

11) p. 14–16
Which of his proposals seem exaggerated, which ones might come true in the fairly near future?

Vorschläge für Klausuren

Textausschnitt 1

Bernard gave his orders in the sharp, rather arrogant and even offensive tone of one who does not feel himself too secure in his superiority. To have dealings with members of the lower castes was always, for Bernard, a most distressing experience. For whatever the cause (and the current gossip about the alcohol in his bloodsurrogate may very
5 likely – for accidents will happen – have been true) Bernard's physique was hardly better than the average Gamma. He stood eight centimetres short of the standard Alpha height and was slender in proportion. Contact with members of the lower castes always reminded him painfully of this physical inadequacy. "I am I, and wish I wasn't"; his self-consciousness was acute and distressing. Each time he found himself looking on the
10 level, instead of downward, into a Delta's face, he felt humiliated. Would the creature treat him with the respect due to his caste? The question haunted him. Not without reason. For Gammas, Deltas, and Epsilons had been to some extent conditioned to associate corporeal mass with social superiority. Indeed, a faint hypnopaedic prejudice in favour of size was universal. Hence the laughter of the women to whom he made propo-
15 sals, the practical joking of his equals among the men. The mockery made him feel an outsider; and feeling an outsider he behaved like one, which increased the prejudice against him and intensified the contempt and hostility aroused by his physical defects. Which in turn increased his sense of being alien and alone. A chronic fear of being slight-ed made him avoid his equals, made him stand, where his inferiors were concerned,
20 self-consciously on his dignity. How bitterly he envied men like Henry Foster and Ben-ito Hoover! Men who never had to shout at an Epsilon to get an order obeyed; men who took their position for granted; men who moved through the caste system as a fish through the water – so utterly at home as to be unaware either of themselves or of the beneficient and comfortable element in which they had their being.
25   (p. 75/76)

I) Translate from line 18–24.

II) *Answer the Questions!*
1) Which part of the novel is the extract taken from? What has happened so far? (4 VP)
2) In line 22 Bernard speaks of the "caste system". What are the different techniques that are applied to establish the caste system, and how are they justified? (8 VP)
3) Here we can observe Bernard in one particular situation
   a) Choose two more situations in the novel which characterize him.
   b) Who is Bernard opposed to, and why? (3 VP/4 VP)
4) a) What does Bernard mean when he says of Foster and Hoover that they're "unaware of themselves"?

b) Which word standing for one of the basic aims in Brave New World is implied in "unaware of themselves"? Explain this term and its importance for Brave New World! (4 VP/4 VP)

5) Bernard suffers from his position as an outsider, but another person in the novel claims "the right to be unhappy". Who is this person? Who is he talking to, and what does he mean by this? (4 VP)

6) In his foreword Huxley says that the Savage "is offered only two alternatives ... insanity on the one hand and lunacy on the other." Interpret Huxley's statement? Do you agree? (4 VP)

Punktverteilung:

Übersetzung:	15 VP
Sprache:	20 VP (Die Fehlerskala bezieht sich auf die Gesamtwortzahl aus allen sechs Fragen)
Inhalt:	35 VP insgesamt (Einzelwertung- siehe Fragen!)

Textausschnitt 2

"The optimum population", said Mustapha Mond, "is modelled on the iceberg — eight-ninths below the water line, one-ninth above."
"And they're happy below the water line?"
"Happier than above it. Happier than your friends here, for example." He pointed.
5 "In spite of that awful, work?"
"Awful? *They* don't find it so. On the contrary, they like it. It's light, it's childishly simple. No strain on the mind or the muscles. Seven and a half hours of mild, unexhausting labour, and then the *soma* ration and games and unrestricted copulation and the feelies. What more can they ask for? True," he added, "they might ask for shorter hours. And
10 of course we could give them shorter hours. Technically, it would be perfectly simple to reduce all lower-caste working hours to three or four a day. But would they be any the happier for that? No, they wouldn't. The experiment was tried, more than a century and a half ago. The whole of Ireland was put on to the four-hour day. What was the result? Unrest and a large increase in the consumption of *soma*; that was all. Those three and a
15 half hours of extra leisure were so far from being a source of happiness, that people felt constrained to take a holiday from them. The Inventions Office is stuffed with plans for labour-saving processes. Thousands of them." Mustapha Mond made a lavish gesture. "And why don't we put them into execution? For the sake of the labourers; it would be sheer cruelty to afflict them with excessive leisure. It's the same with agriculture. We
20 could synthesize every morsel of food, if we wanted to. But we don't. We prefer to keep a third of the population on the land. For their own sakes — because it takes *longer* to get food out of the land than out of a factory. Besides, we have our stability to think of. We don't want to change. Every change is a menace to stability. That's another reason why we're so chary of applying new inventions. Every discovery in pure science is potentially
25 subversive; even science must sometimes be treated as a possible enemy. Yes, even science."
(p. 222/23)

I) Translate from line 20–26.

II) *Answer the Questions!*
1) Which part of the novel is this extract taken from? Who is Mustapha Mond talking to, and why? (50–80 Wö / 4 VP)
2) What does Mustapha Mond hint at when he speaks of the "iceberg"? What are the (three) main principles of the system of "Brave New World", and how is its society supposed to function? (ca. 150 Wö / 10 VP)
3) In line 8 Mond speaks of "soma" (a) and "copulation" (sex) (b)
   a) What is the official function of "soma"? Are there any persons who are exceptions from the rule? (60–80 Wö / 3 VP)
   b) To what extent can the relationship between Bernard and Lenina be said to exemplify the role of sex in "Brave New World"? (3 VP)
   c) The Brave New Worlders have created their own God. What are the two names they've given him, and what are the theories associated with these names? (ca. 80 Wö / 5 VP)
   d) Why have they not kept our Christian God? (ca. 80 Wö / 4 VP)
5) In line 25 Mustapha Mond sees science as a "possible enemy" of the system. Why? (ca. 60 Wö / 3 VP)
6) Are there any other things that might menace the stability of the system? (ca. 40 Wö / 3 VP)

Punktverteilung:
Übersetzung: 15 VP
Sprache: 20 VP. (Die Fehlerskala bezieht sich auf die Gesamtwortzahl aus allen sechs Fragen)
Inhalt: 35 VP (insgesamt; Einzelwertung siehe Fragen)

Benutzte Literatur

Raymond Aron, Fortschritt ohne Ende. Über die Zukunft der Industriegesellschaft. Gütersloh 1970

Wayne C. Booth, The Rhetoric of Fiction, Chicago 1961

Marjorie Boulton, The Anatomy of Prose, London 1954

Charles Brenner, Grundzüge der Psychoanalyse, Frankfurt/Main 1976

Charles Brenner, Praxis der Psychoanalyse, Frankfurt/Main 1979

Jenni Calder, Huxley – Brave New World and Orwell – Nineteen Eighty Four, London 1976

E. M. Cioran, Geschichte und Utopie, Stuttgart 1979

François de Closets, Vorsicht Fortschritt. Über die Zukunft der Industriegesellschaft. Frankfurt/Main 1971

Ralf Dahrendorf, Pfade aus Utopia. Zu einer Neuorientierung der soziologischen Analyse, in: H. Albert (Hrsg.): Theorie und Realität, Tübingen 1964

Die Geningenieure spielen mit dem Code des Lebens", in: Bild der Wissenschaft, Juli 1979, S. 30–42

Robert C. Elliot, The Shape of Utopia. Studies in a Literary Genre. Chicago & London 1970

Dorothy van Ghent, The English Novel. Form and Function. New York 1953

Ernesto Grassi/Walter Hess (Hrsg.), Der utopische Staat (Morus / Campanella / Bacon), Reinbek 1962

Jost Herbig, Die Geningenieure, München/Wien 1978

Aldous Huxley, Brave New World Revisited, London 1974 (first printed in 1958)

Insight II, Analyses of Modern British Literature, ed. by John V. Hagopian and Martin Dolch. Frankfurt/Main 1971

Eugène Ionesco, Of Utopianism and Intellectuals. Aus: Encounter, February 1978, pp. 36–37

Wolf Lepenies, Melancholie und Gesellschaft, Frankfurt/Main 1969

Jerome Meckier, Aldous Huxley: Utopie im Kontrapunkt und Wunschtraum, in: W. Erzgräber (Hrsg.): Englische Literatur von Wilde bis Beckett (Interpretationen 9), Frankfurt 1970

George Orwell, Nineteen Eighty-Four, Penguin Books Harmondsworth 1979 (first published in 1949)

Hugh J. Silverman, From Utopia/Dystopia to Heterotopia. An interpretative topology. Lecture given at the World Congress of Sociology in Uppsalla in 1978

B. F. Skinner, Futurum Zwei (Walden Two). Vision einer aggressionsfreien Gesellschaft. Hamburg 1972. (Originalausgabe: Walden Two, New York 1948)

David Stafford-Clark, What Freud really said, Penguin Books Harmondsworth 1965

Jonathan Swift, Gulliver's Travels, Penguin Books Harmondsworth 1968, (first published in 1726)

Alvin Toffler, Future Shock, London 1976, pp. 421–423

Yves Velan, Soft Gulag, Köln 1980

John B. Watson, Behaviorism, Toronto 1970 (first published in 1924)

Evelyn Waugh, The Loved One, Penguin Books Harmondsworth 1979 (first published in 1948)

Leichter lernen, lieber lernen. Also Klett.

Lektürehilfen

Lektürehilfen Fitzgerald
»The Great Gatsby«
ISBN 3-12-922238-3

Lektürehilfen Golding
»Lord of the Flies«
ISBN 3-12-922222-7

Lektürehilfen Hemingway
»A Farewell to Arms«
ISBN 3-12-922235-9

Lektürehilfen Huxley
»Brave New World«
ISBN 3-12-922224-3

Lektürehilfen Miller
»Death of a Salesman«
ISBN 3-12-922228-6

Lektürehilfen Miller
»The Crucible«
ISBN 3-12-922236-7

Lektürehilfen Orwell
»Animal Farm«
ISBN 3-12-922226-X

Lektürehilfen Orwell
»1984«
ISBN 3-12-922225-1

Lektürehilfen Salinger
»The Catcher in the Rye«
ISBN 3-12-922221-9

Lektürehilfen Shakespeare
»Hamlet«
ISBN 3-12-922232-4

Lektürehilfen Shakespeare
»Julius Caesar«
ISBN 3-12-922229-4

Lektürehilfen Shakespeare
»Macbeth«
ISBN 3-12-922223-5

Lektürehilfen Shakespeare
»Romeo and Juliet«
ISBN 3-12-922234-0

Lektürehilfen Steinbeck
»Of Mice and Men«
ISBN 3-12-922233-2

Lektürehilfen Williams
»The Glass Menagerie«
»A Streetcar Named Desire«
ISBN 3-12-922231-6

Stundenblätter Englisch